A Swan in Heaven
Conversations Between Two Worlds

Terri Daniel
with
Danny Mandell

A Note About the Swan Magic in This Book

One day during Danny's 11th year on earth, I watched a documentary about the firefighters who'd battled the blaze at the World Trade Center on September 11, 2001. Those who'd fought the fire and survived felt unbearable grief about the partners who'd fought beside them and perished. Their grief was complicated by guilt, and so deep was this grief/guilt conjunction that some of the survivors chose to have images of their fallen friends tattooed on their backs. These were much more than muddy impressions haphazardly etched onto a shoulder or a bicep. They were finely detailed, larger-than-life portraits that covered their backs from shoulder to shoulder, waist to neck. The firefighters said, "This way I will have my partner's spirit with me every day of my life."

Inspired by this, I wanted a tattoo representing Danny's spirit to become a permanent part of my own body. I wanted a symbol of his soul to watch over me, perched on my shoulder like a guardian angel. But what kind of symbol could accurately represent him?

At the time he was still able to talk, so I asked him, "If you could be any animal, what would it be?" And he said, without hesitation, "A swan."

What an interesting choice. I didn't even think he knew what swans were, and I was pretty sure he'd never actually seen one. I expected a dinosaur or a tiger, maybe a dolphin or a wolf or a superhero. Something a pre-pubescent boy would relate to. But a *swan?*

I questioned him again and again about it, but he didn't budge.

One week later I was the proud bearer of a bright and beautiful swan, tattooed in vibrant colors on my left shoulder. I was beginning to learn how to trust Danny's wisdom in such matters. And in the months that followed, as I researched "swan medicine," I found that Danny, as always, knew exactly what he was talking about.

On the eve of submitting this manuscript to the publisher for the second edition of this book, Danny spoke to my psychic friend Rebecca, and said, "When I told my mom about the swan, it was meant to represent *her,* because she is the one who is dancing between dimensions. I chose that symbol because our work together is Swan Magic. The whole point of our lives together was transformation, and the whole country went through a transformation at the time I made that comment. Swan medicine and its story should be like a precious white cloud that surrounds the reader from the first words. So please insert this explanation at the front of the book."

LITTLE SWAN IN DREAMTIME

Little Swan flew through the Dreamtime, looking for the future. She rested for a moment in the coolness of the pond, looking for a way to find the entry point to the future. This was a moment of confusion for Swan, as she knew that she had happened into the Dreamtime by accident. This was her first flight alone and she was a bit concerned by the Dreamtime landscape.

As Swan looked high above Sacred Mountain, she saw the biggest swirling black hole she had ever seen. Dragonfly came flying by, and Swan stopped him to ask about the black hole. Dragonfly said, "Swan, that is the doorway to the other planes of imagination. I have been guardian of the illusion for many, many moons. If you want to enter there, you would have to ask permission and *earn* the right."

Swan was not so sure that she wanted to enter the black hole. She asked Dragonfly what was necessary for her to earn entry. Dragonfly replied, "You must be willing to accept whatever the future holds as it is presented, without trying to change Great Spirit's plan." Swan looked at her ugly little duckling body and then answered, "I will be happy to abide by Great Spirit's plan. I won't fight the currents of the black hole. I will *surrender* to the flow of the spiral and *trust* what I am shown."

Dragonfly was very happy with Swan's answer and began to spin the magic to break the pond's illusion. Suddenly, Swan was engulfed by a whirlpool in the center of the pond.

Swan reappeared many days later, but now she was graceful and white and long-necked. Dragonfly was stunned! "Swan, what happened to you?" he exclaimed. Swan smiled and said, "Dragonfly, I learned to surrender my body to the power of Great Spirit and was taken to where the future lives. I saw many wonders high on Sacred Mountain and because of my faith and my acceptance I have been changed. I have learned to accept the state of grace." Dragonfly was very happy for Swan.

Swan told Dragonfly many of the wonders beyond the illusion. Through her healing and her acceptance of the state of grace, she was given the right to enter the Dreamtime.

So it is that we learn to surrender to the grace of the rhythm of the universe, and slip from our physical bodies into the Dreamtime. Swan medicine teaches us to be at one with all the planes of consciousness, and to trust in Great Spirit's protection.

"Swan Medicine" is reprinted from the MEDICINE CARDS with permission of Jamie Sams and David Carson, authors. Illustration by Angela Werneke, published by St. Martin's Press. Copyright 1988 and 1999.

A Swan in Heaven
Conversations Between Two Worlds

Terri Daniel
with Danny Mandell

359 N. Locust Lane
Sisters, OR. 97759
541-549-4004
www.SwanInHeaven.com

A Swan in Heaven:
Conversations Between Two Worlds

Books may be purchased from local and online booksellers
or directly from the publisher:

First House Press
359 N. Locust Lane
Sisters, OR. 97759
541-549-4004

www.SwanInHeaven.com

ISBN: 978-0-9623062-5-9

I dedicate this book to divine energy,
to God, the guides, the angels and the messengers
who have so lovingly directed me.

But above all I dedicate this work to Danny,
my greatest gift, my teacher, my co-author
and my constant companion.

ACKNOWLEGEMENTS

Immense gratitude to many special friends:

Amy Sorrel, Danny's one true love.

Charlene Lee for walks, talks and a case of wine.

Nicole, who became a big sister
even though she was physically a younger one.

Jack, with love and forgiveness.

Erika Snowden for her profound gift of unconditional love.

Jim Mandell for making Danny possible.

Judy Gibson for being literate, attentive and attuned.

Lee Green and hospice workers everywhere.

Michael Sherick for the moon and stars.*

Rebecca Covington, who introduced me to channeling and so
generously made her guides available to me.

Scott, Ocallah and Mariah, who helped me connect
when I doubted my own abilities.

The D-9, my earth angels.

The people in Alabama who loved us,
and those who've forgotten us.

Gratitude and love to many others in Danny's soul family:

Abigail, Jeff, Juliana, Alex & Barbara Mandell; Andrea Morrison MD; Annette, Joey & Lorraina; Ashley Dodd; Basil Scafidi; Caprice Fowler; Carly Foster; Cathy Horne; CCS; Chris Johnson; Chris McGee; Colina Middle School; CRS in Alabama; Edith, Carl & Aaron Hinrichs; Fairhope High School; Fairhope Middle School; Jan Perry; Jenny & Aaron Claire; Jessica Eddins & baby Daniel; John Cruz; Karen Bounds; Katie & Doug Cavanaugh; Kelsey Collins; Keri Bowers; Laura Cleary; Laura & Delene; Linda Enfinger; Lindsay Roberts; Lisa & Maddie Simmons; Lisa Dunaway; Lynn Woodward; Margaret & Sydney Clanagan; Marilyn & Marty Rose; Mary Van Antwerp; Mary Mac; Matt Kramer; Melanie Tew; Michel Philippart MD; Neil, Lori & Jordan; Noelle Altamura; Paul Fisk; Paul Maertens MD; Paula Drummond MD; Robin Clark & family; Shelley & Warren Yonker; Sheri Moran; Siggie & Virginia; Stuart, Kimberly & their children; Susie Camanetti; Tina Ebsen; Tina McGough; Tyler Nutt … and anybody else who's ever felt the power of Danny's love.

*Special thanks to Michael Sherick for the cover photograph of the *"The Cygnus Wall of Star Formation."* The part of the North America nebula shown spans about 15 light years and lies about 1,500 light years away toward the constellation of Cygnus (The Swan).

Cover image copyright 2007 Michael Sherick—
www. imagingtheheavens.com

Special thanks to Lori Justice-Shocket and Pam Hunter for cover design

PART ONE: EARTH

PART TWO: HEAVEN

PART ONE

Earth

INTRODUCTION

Two years before my son Danny died at age 16 from a rare, degenerative metabolic disorder, I began developing some minor psychic abilities and learned to channel angels, guides and other entities. I was far from expert at this, but did possess a highly-tuned intuition that made it possible for me to interpret dreams, Tarot cards and other transmissions with enough confidence to heed their guidance for myself and to occasionally assist others. I had no idea at the time that I was in training for the remarkable experience of receiving messages from Danny after his death.

As my telepathic skills were increasing, Danny's ability to speak was diminishing. Before the onset of his illness he was a normal boy with superior language skills, but as the disease progressed he gradually lost the power of speech along with most of his other physical abilities. During the latter part of his illness he could express himself well enough to let me know if he was hungry or cold, and respond to simple questions with one-word answers. But by the time he died he had been completely without words for nearly two years, and we had learned to communicate using a natural form of telepathy, similar to the way mothers communicate with their pre-verbal infants.

Not more than an hour after Danny took his last breath, while I lay on his bed holding his limp body in my arms and crying into his silent chest, I had my first vision of him on the "other side." For the previous five years he'd been wheelchair-bound, his spine and limbs cramped from the deterioration of his muscles, and it had been a long time since I'd been able to gather his body up in my arms with any sort of fluidity. But at this moment I could at last hold him like that, with his body unwound and his soul released. The vision came instantly, as clear as can be, and it was so funny that I laughed out loud. I'd asked him to show me a picture of where he was at that moment, and I instantly saw him looking like James Dean from the movie *Rebel Without a Cause*, wearing blue jeans with rolled up cuffs and a white t-shirt. He was wading in shallow water, kicking his legs in front of him and laughing.

In subsequent visits his appearance changed. Sometimes he'd have ridiculously long legs as if he were walking on stilts, still wading in water, kicking his legs around and enjoying his beautiful new body. At other times he loomed large in front of me like a Macy's parade balloon, laughing and bouncing through the sky. Most of the time though, he looks just like himself, only older, taller, and usually wearing jeans, sometimes with a black t-shirt instead of a white one. Sometimes he appears to be about 20 years old, but at other times he's wearing the face he had at 11. He tells me that he appears younger when he's in "learning mode," studying with the great teachers who are assisting him on the other side.

There are many beautiful aspects to our inter-dimensional relationship, not the least of which is that for the first time ever, I can have adult conversations with him. Before the disease took his voice, he was a little boy and talked of little boy things. Now we converse like two wise old sages, but he is far older and wiser than I. He told me we would write this book together and that we'd planned it long before we were mother and son in this incarnation. He now converses with me regularly, and at times the messages come so quickly that I can't take dictation fast enough, while at other times there are periods with no contact at all. I learned from Danny that the no-contact periods usually happen when I'm caught up in my emotions and tormented by the dramas in my personal life. Whenever I can't see my way through anger, blame or fear, Danny is harder to reach. He once told me he would "allow" me five minutes to vent prior to our conversations, and then I'd have to release everything and open my heart to peace. By understanding that he's attracted to the energy of love and forgiveness and repelled by the energy of fear and unrest, I was motivated to begin looking at myself unflinchingly, and as a result my life began to transform.

Wisdom from non-physical guides is available to everybody on earth, not just prophets, psychics or a chosen few. It's always accessible and never changes, and anyone who asks for it can receive it easily. In fact, the hardest part is believing how easy it really is. It's simple universal truth, presented with no judgment, no dogma and no agenda. When studying the popular channeled books by Edgar Cayce, Jane Roberts, James Van Praagh and Neale Donald Walsch, one notices that there's very little variation from one book to the next, and that there is a stunning consistency running through all the material. Lesser-known books like *Child of Eternity*, channeled by a nine year-old autistic girl, tell the identical story in the same language of gentle, unconditional love. They speak of loving entities who guide us from other realms, and they dismiss the fear-based concept of angry, judgmental gods.

People are starving for this kind of material. We seek believable, non-judgmental explanations for our experiences on earth, and alternatives to the fear and disempowerment many of us experienced in the churches of our childhoods. Remarkably, all the answers are there simply for the asking, requiring nothing more than an open heart and the understanding that we are much more than these interim physical forms. Emotional and spiritual education is available to us in many forms from many sources, beyond books, schools and human experience. There are eager teachers like Danny in other realms waiting with infinite patience for us to tune in and start listening.

Since all channeled books say basically the same thing, at one point I became concerned that our book wouldn't be saying anything *new*. But Danny set me straight on that, and I was surprised at how insistent he was that our book have a very specific slant. He told me that the book would not be merely about the journey of the soul, but would explain high-level spiritual concepts through an examination of *intimate relationships* and the power of forgiveness to transform them.

An unlikely topic for a teenage boy, but not surprising considering that Danny spent the entire duration of his illness in the midst of my emotionally -- and sometimes physically -- violent marriage to his stepfather.

Against a backdrop of chaos and instability, Danny's message of personal responsibility, forgiveness and acceptance teaches us that there can be no such thing as abuse, because from a spiritual perspective, there are no victims and no perpetrators. All relationships are created and agreed to by the participants, via soul contracts and growth agreements made prior to our incarnations on earth. Danny's perceptions of life, death and disability shine like a beacon and cut like a knife, getting to the heart of the matter and guiding us toward higher ways of understanding ourselves and our personal relationships.

It has been awkward, agonizing and humbling for me to write about the unsightly details of my marriage within the squeaky-clean context of Danny's messages, and I struggled with doubt every step of the way. But in the moments when I was most unsure, when I asked myself, "do I really need to include this? Do I sound like a victim? Am I being too judgmental and blaming?" I would stop writing, go into my meditation room and ask for clarification from my guides (Danny has introduced me to several who are on the other side with him). What you see here is the material that made it through this cosmic scrutiny process.

So at the behest of my son the sage, I reveal myself and my marriage to the world, realizing that Danny knew exactly what he was doing when he chose the life he shared with his stepfather and me. He lived a life of selflessness and vision, silent and helpless in the middle of a marriage that many psychologists would define as abusive. A normal child could have spoken out, expressed his pain or run away. But Danny was a master of stillness, and chose instead to "be" with the unease, radiating love and forgiveness without a word.

Did Danny's non-verbal condition provide a mirror for my own suppressed communications in the marriage? Certainly. Did learning to let Danny's voice come through me for spiritual teaching release me from my own silence? Absolutely. Do we have something to teach others about finding their voices, understanding emotional chaos from a higher perspective, and healing broken hearts? I hope so.

Danny *knows* so.

1. The First Day

"When I was four years old I used to tell you that I came from Jupiter, and it made me happy that you not only believed me, but asked me for details and seemed truly interested. It was hard to describe in the limited language of a four year-old, but I can explain it to you now. I was aware of having another home and another family somewhere far away. The memory faded as I got older, but when I got sick and my body began to fail, I could see visions of that home again. It pulled me closer and closer, and I knew I had to release my body in order to get back there, because it's the real home where we all come from and where we all really live. This is the most important thing that we in Heaven are trying to teach... how to release the illusions, negativities and beliefs of the body in order to be open to the truths of Heaven."

Danny, ten days after his death

I've been instructed to start telling the story beginning with the day of Danny's death, because that is exactly where the story begins. But I'm actually going to start a few days earlier, on the day when I began to feel myself becoming open in a way I had never experienced or expected.

On this day things started to flow easily and effortlessly, and the flow encompassed everything around me, including the presence and placement of people and events, a sense of being and doing exactly what I was supposed to be and do, and the knowledge that I would soon be permanently, magnificently changed. This subtle and slow-growing shift in awareness actually began about three months before Danny made the final journey out of his body, when he cleverly orchestrated a "dress rehearsal" to prepare us for his impending transition.

The details don't matter other than to say that he was in the hospital with dehydration and pneumonia, and during this time I created sacred space around him in every way I knew how. He couldn't tell me in words, but I knew his intention was to allow himself to be patched up by doctors just this one time, just long enough to get us used to the idea that his body was no longer viable and he was ready to leave it. In the weeks that followed, he led

5

me on a journey of gratitude and acceptance, in which both of us came to embrace his death with joy and relief.

The week he was in the hospital I had a psychic reading with my dear friend Rebecca Covington, a gifted medium who channels a group of non-physical entities known as "Elishevaa." I'd been having readings with Rebecca since 1998, and over the years these readings have not only guided me, they educated and primed me for the emergence of my own abilities in this area. In this particular reading Elishevaa told me that my role in the process of Danny's death was to act as a midwife, assisting him with his birth into the next world, and that this role was pristine and elevated, to be protected and revered at all times. Elishevaa's exact words were:

Danny does not wish to exist in a netherworld imprisoned in his body, and he feels that his work is done. But he does not want to cause you pain, and feels he is the only joy in your life. Do not become overly emotional when with him, for it burdens him in ways he cannot express, but be honest, as you have, that you will be sad, but eventually fine, and how you look forward to him laughing and running and playing and talking, and having him eventually communicating through you and what wonderful things you'll talk about. For now you will be bathed in light and allow nothing else into your existence or awareness for the sake of Danny. Nothing else will exist for you. The ritual of transition begins and it is up to you to bring only light and peace into the circle of honor here. As though no two people exist in the world except for you and Danny - no different than childbirth.

That meant not only creating peaceful space for Danny, but also doing the same for myself by keeping my heart both protected and open at the same time, which was no small task. I knew I needed to release as much fear, doubt, anger and negativity as possible, so along with my usual meditation practices, I worked on disengaging from the intense strife in my marriage. With Danny's death approaching, the stress levels were higher than usual, and the pain and grief I'd been anticipating for so long were beginning to surface. I was fearful about how this additional burden would affect the volatile interactions which had been the hallmark of my relationship with my husband during our nine years together.

My husband Jack was not the type who could deal directly with strong emotions, and his pattern was to keep his feelings inside until they'd inevitably break through in bursts of irrational anger, odd behaviors and occasional physical violence. I didn't want Danny to spend his last months on earth experiencing this kind of the turmoil, so in order to maintain a semblance of peace, I decided to withdraw completely from Jack and keep my thoughts, needs and concerns about Danny to myself in an attempt to avoid as much conflict as possible. This wasn't difficult to do, since Jack and I had already been sleeping separately for most of the past year, and I'd long since stopped trying to communicate with him about anything more sensitive than mundane household business. I knew that proximity to him would lead to angry outbursts and hurtful words, and I vowed that Danny would never have to witness such things again.

Danny's transition had indeed begun, and among other things, I struggled with guilt, wondering if he'd decided to die merely to escape the chaos and sadness in our home. When Rebecca asked Elishevaa about this for me, they gave me a metaphysical slap on the wrist for thinking that anybody could influence another's choice about when or why to die.

I spent Danny's last few weeks reminiscing with him about our life together and the beautiful times we'd shared, while showing him pictures in our family photo albums (he had a hard time focusing on the pictures because as I learned later, his eyes were drying out from dehydration and he could not see very well). I also spent a lot of time lying next to him in his bed, whispering to him about the beauty of "Heaven" as I perceive it. I told him how he'd meet up with members of his soul family... friends and loved ones he'd forgotten during this incarnation but would remember with great love the instant he saw them. And I assured him that I would be there too, because all of us here on earth are capable of vibrating in more than one dimension simultaneously, and though I'd still be in a physical body, we would be together on the other side at the same time.

Little did I know how true that would turn out to be.

I must preface this next section by saying that Danny was not my biological child. My previous husband Jim and I adopted Danny at birth. His birth mother was a spirited 26 year-old girl named Erika Snowden, who had a beautiful open soul and an extraordinary set of parents named Paula and Frank. Via an introduction through a mutual friend, Jim and I met Erika and her parents during Erika's seventh month of pregnancy. It was love at first sight for all of us, and we began to formulate a spiritual and legal agreement for the adoption of Erika's baby boy. The name she had chosen for him was *Morgan Snowden*, a Celtic name that not only reflected her heritage, but also reflected a culture to which I'd been inexplicably drawn for decades. We changed his name when we adopted him of course, but I've since added "Snowden" to honor Erika for giving me the greatest gift I've ever received. We supported her during her pregnancy and all of us were in the delivery room together during Danny's birth. We stayed in touch for several years afterwards, recognizing the importance of our bond as a soul family, but eventually we lost track of her.

Erika's mother Paula -- Danny's biological grandmother -- died at age 46 from a surgical complication two years after Danny was born. She was in a coma for several days before she died, and when I went to visit her in the hospital I brought one of Danny's baby blankets with me. When I laid it on Paula's stomach, to the amazement of everybody in the room, she grabbed it with her hand and held it tightly. Later than night, around 11 pm, two year-old Danny woke up crying and inconsolable, and it took me hours to comfort him. He had been an extraordinary infant who started sleeping through the night at five weeks dd, and always slept easily and peacefully. But on this night he woke up nearly hysterical, and the next morning I learned that Paula had died at 11 pm. I knew without a doubt that she'd done a "fly by" to visit him. Their special connection was now established.

Fast-forward 14 years and Danny is now five days away from his own death. I hadn't thought much about Paula over the years, but when I showed Danny her picture in the photo album, her presence filled the room. As it turned out, she was preparing to do another fly by.

Paula's visitations started earlier that day when I got a call from an acquaintance inviting me to a chanting group she was hosting that evening. I really didn't want to go. I wasn't interested in chanting and had never done it before, so I told her that my child was sick and I couldn't leave him. Literally 30 seconds after I hung up the phone, Lisa, one of Danny's hired in-home aides, called and said, "I can come by and stay with Dan for a while today if you'd like to get out and go somewhere."

So I knew I was supposed to go to this chanting thing.

I arrived there to find about a dozen people I'd never met before (rare in our small town), and a man named John led us in several Buddhist chants for healing, compassion and heart opening. I'd never chanted before, and found it distracting, because when I meditate I *want* to listen to the cosmic debris in my mind. That's where I hear the voices of my guides, and chanting drowns it out, which may be the goal for many people, but not for me.

So I decided to stop chanting and just listen to the others, and to my delight I found that their sounds created a vibration that actually helped me open up a conduit to messages trying to come through. Sure enough, Paula showed up and started talking to me. She said that she was coming to take Danny home (when the group was chanting "Om" it sounded like "home") and that she, Erika and I were a trinity of goddess/mother energy, all three shepherding Danny through this remarkable incarnation of his.

While I was basking in Paula's loving light, the chanting ended and John put a CD on, telling us to listen to the song and meditate on goddess energy (there are truly no coincidences). He played the most beautiful recording of Ave Maria that I'd ever heard, and all through the song Paula's presence filled me with peace. I asked her why I had not seen her before, during the years of Danny's illness, and she told me it was because she was specifically there to be a guide for Danny's death, and had not been needed until now.

LIFE ENDS... AND BEGINS

Five days later Danny died. He was lying in his bed on a beautiful memorial quilt that a group of friends had created together for exactly this purpose. My dear friend Lee Green, the bereavement specialist at our hospice agency, called it his "journey blanket." It is now my journey blanket too, because I wrap myself in its radiant energy whenever I need to feel Danny physically close to me.

On that morning and all through the previous night, Danny slept deeply, his lungs emitting a gurgling sound with each breath. He'd been sleeping curled up on his side all night, and when our hospice nurse, Jake, came for his morning visit, he rolled Danny onto his back to look into his eyes and check his vital signs. Danny was breathing and gurgling peacefully, but his eyes were doing something I'd never seen before. They were open and looking up at the ceiling, not directly above him, but a few inches behind him, staring at something unseen to the rest of us. Jake recognized this look and declared that Danny was in the process of "separating" and was most likely unaware of anything going on around him. Jake said that Danny would probably live no more than 24 hours. That look in Danny's eyes still haunts me and fascinates me (I have since learned that this look is common in dying people), and sometimes when I meditate I focus my eyes in the same way, trying to see what Danny was seeing.

I had less than 24 hours left to comfort my sweet boy, to feel the final beats of his heart and to lay my head next to his so I could feel the last of his warm breaths on my cheek. I scrambled around all morning taking care of little household tasks, frantically trying to get things done so I could spend some quiet time lying by his side. All my friends and family members knew Danny was dying and had nothing but the best intentions, but the constantly ringing phone and the steady stream of people coming to the door drove me crazy. There were a thousand distractions and fires to put out before I could settle down and spend time with Danny. I even spent an hour finishing up some work for a client because I knew I wouldn't be able to focus on work during the weeks to come.

Finally things got quiet and I went in to be with Danny.

"Hi baby, I'm here now," I said. "I'm sorry I was so busy all morning, but I'm here now."

I stroked his hair, moistened his lips with a glycerin swab and thought about putting on some music, but changed my mind, thinking that he was probably already hearing the music of the spheres.

And that's when I realized that I could no longer hear the gurgling sound. I must have been there tending to him for a full minute before I noticed that he wasn't breathing.

Danny did what people often do; he waited until I was busy elsewhere to finalize his transition. As I'd been taught by many hospice workers, my presence close to him would have held him here. Although I knew this intellectually, I felt terrible that I didn't spend those last hours by his side. *What was I thinking?* How could I have chosen to straighten up the house and do work for a client while my child was dying? Later that night I lamented to my friend Edith, a recent widow, "This wasn't the way I wanted it to be." And she said, "It was the way *he* wanted it to be."

It was weeks later before I finally understood that Paula and many other guides were with him during those hours, and that he most certainly did not die alone. Nobody ever does.

Jack's daughter Nicole, who is the same age as Danny and lovingly embraced her role as Danny's step-sister, lived with her mother 50 miles away, but came to stay with us during Danny's last days. When we realized that Danny had died, Nicole and I held each other and cried while Jack checked Danny's pupils and other indicators trying to figure out how long he'd been "gone." We determined that it had happened only in the last five minutes, as we retraced our steps leading up to that moment.

Jack, Nicole and I lay on the bed cuddled up with Danny's body for a long time. We dressed him in a special shirt Jack had made several months earlier, which had the handicapped logo on it with the words "Life Rolls On." We laid flowers on his chest and all around him. Then I shooed everyone away so I could spend some time alone with him.

I held him closer than I'd been able to hold him in a long time, because his cramped, disabled body had been so difficult to handle, and now it was pliant and relaxed. I held him and cried, asking him to show me a picture of what it was like wherever he was located at that moment.

Instantly, I saw an image of Danny wearing jeans with the cuffs rolled up and a white t-shirt, and he looked like James Dean in the 1950s movie *Rebel Without a Cause*. He was standing in (on?) water and kicking his legs out in front of him, and he was laughing. He was ecstatic! My crying turned to amazement, and I held his body even closer, laughing and sobbing and saying, "thank you, thank you, thank you, my darling boy."

About an hour later, Amy and Lisa, our two in-home aides who also worked in Danny's classroom at school (I hesitate to call them aides because they are part of the family and more like sisters) showed up, and the four of us -- Amy, Lisa, Nicole and I -- spent the rest of the time cuddling with Danny, petting him, talking, laughing and crying. At one point one of us was sitting on each corner of the bed, each caressing a hand or a foot, and it seemed quite humorous, dividing Danny's extremities like that. None of us could stop touching him. And it was funny, because it didn't look much different than a typical day in Danny's life, with him lying on his bed surrounded by adoring females holding his hands and massaging his feet. The only difference was that *Sponge Bob Square Pants* wasn't on the TV and Danny wasn't in his body.

We kept him there with us for five hours before calling the funeral home to take his body away. I'd arranged to donate his brain to a research program, and just before the attendants pulled the blanket up over his face, I held his head in my hands and said a prayer that his brain would help find a cure for this dreadful disease.

We gathered, shell-shocked in the front yard, and watched them drive away. It was about 6 pm, and we spent the rest of the evening sitting in the living room telling stories about Danny, so bonded by this experience and so comforted by each other's presence that nobody wanted to leave the room. There was food in the kitchen but nobody wanted to separate from the group to deal with something as mundane as food. Edith showed up a bit later and joined our little circle, perfect and unbroken until 11 pm. Nobody wanted to go home.

I slept in Danny's bed that night, on his journey blanket, and Jack joined me there at some point during the night. There was a beautiful, peaceful energy in Danny's room, but the rest of the house was cold and lifeless.

In the morning I called Rebecca, asking her to contact Elishevaa for news of Danny's journey. They said:

Loved ones, as difficult as it is to celebrate, it truly is a time of celebration! It is as though one has been jailed unfairly and the DNA has been found to belong to another, and he has been freed! He can dance and laugh and shout and feel and he is delighting in this glorious new body! He is saying, "Do not be sad! You cannot realize how soon we will be together again!" And it is true the picture that you have in your mind–he gave it to you as a gift, the 'James Dean' picture, because it is to make you laugh and give you joy and a sight of truth! He is bathed in light, and he is still very close and will stay close for a time, before making a journey to the Hall of Records and a time of review and study. He will spend time comforting you and others, and 'looking over' his life from the earth perspective. Allow yourself this time to talk to him and spend time in his presence, and share in his joy. But dear sister, also allow yourself a time to grieve, and do not be hard on yourself for doing so.

DANNY SPEAKS (AND TRIES ON SHOES)

The next day I was lying on Dan's bed wrapped in his journey blanket when to my astonishment, he spoke to me and showed me another image of himself. This time he had long legs as if he was walking on stilts like one of those circus clowns that dresses up as Uncle Sam, and he was walking in shallow water again, kicking his legs up and splashing around. He looked to be very mature, a few years older than his own age, and he was still wearing those jeans, but this time he was also wearing the LIFE ROLLS ON shirt.

I couldn't believe how lucky I was to have actually seen him twice! I asked, "Is that you? Can you talk to me?"

And he started talking in a voice that was different than the voice he had here before he'd lost the ability to speak. It was an older voice, and he said, "Yes, you are hearing me."

And of course my first thought, so typically human, was to fear that I'd lose him, so I said, "Will this stay? Will you stay with me?"

He said, "You will hear me this easily most of the time, when you can clear the conduit. You've been studying and working and doing much to prepare yourself, and now that you have the techniques for calming and receiving, I will come to you whenever you do the steps to take the noise and clutter out of the way. This is one way I can help you remove some of the agitation in your life, because you'll have a motivation for keeping it away."

I was pulled back to earth by thoughts of calling Rebecca to ask Elishevaa if what I had just seen and heard was real. Danny must have heard that thought, because he laughed and said, "I know you need validation, so I'll wait right here while you check in with Rebecca."

This is what Elishevaa said:

We recommend that you begin a journal, or free-flowing thoughts with no attention to order, beginning now. Your thoughts and reflections of the last few weeks especially, along with your experiences of Danny's new experiences now, will be helpful to many others in the future. Your future is beginning NOW. Your grieving process will not be 'normal' (what about your life has ever been normal? You won't be starting "normal" now, loved one), and your process, along with the connection and descriptions of Danny's process, will be unusual and wonderful for others to experience eventually as well.

Because the visions, lessons, and thoughts will come sometimes as a flood, other times as quick revelations, you will never remember them all if you do not start an accounting now. And you will regret losing them if you think you will write them down later. It will also be part of your healing to write them. Yes, we validate all that you are hearing, seeing, you will even be smelling. You will have many sensory experiences as he 'hangs around' and enjoys being, like Pinocchio, a 'real boy' for a while. And even when he does begin his studies so to speak, he will be 'on call' on a very simple duality, such as we are. But this very visceral experience will be highly personal and last for quite some time, do not worry about losing it, for it has only begun.

Danny is very, very excited. There is just no other way to describe it. He is goofing around with the size of his legs, kind of like the old Stretch Armstrong toys. He can do anything he wants, and it's an absolute delight, and there is no one he would rather share this with than you. We also suggest that you cut and paste our words with the

13

words of your reflections and the words of Danny so that you do not forget the validation of Heaven, Read and re-read what we have said, to help you as you mold and confirm and integrate the many levels of information that are coming to you at once.

During the three days that followed, strange and comical things started to happen. I kept seeing Danny as a circus clown on stilts, and then one day I got an email from my friend Melissa, who said, "Danny is with some of my favorite people, including my wonderful daddy who as a boy was an acrobat in the circus. He just taught Danny how to do a cartwheel …what adventures they will have together!"

Melissa knew nothing about my circus clown vision. And neither did Edith, who later in the week invited me to attend a lecture with her on the topic of, believe it or not, P.T. Barnum.

And just to drive the point home (because Danny, the guides and angels were working hard to convince me that this was real), Danny helped find a lost cat. I was on the phone with my friend Mary, telling her about my contact with Danny, and she said, half kidding, "ask him if he can find my neighbor's cat. We've been searching for it all day."

So I hung up the phone, concentrated for a minute, and saw a vision of Danny standing there with my own cat, Maui. The vision lasted for only a split second, but five minutes later Mary called me back to say that the cat had just shown up at the neighbor's door!

The next day I was at the airport waiting for the arrival of my mother and my lifelong friend Shelley, both of whom had flown in to help with the memorial service and the sad, surreal tasks that follow the death of a loved one. I was in the airport restroom and decided to call for Dan to visit me. He showed up immediately in front of me, and this time, with his long legs, he was wearing a pair of white sneakers. It had been a couple of years since he'd worn anything but socks because his feet had become too twisted and contorted for shoes. But he was now showing me a picture of himself trying on different types of shoes, reveling in his newfound ability to wear them.

Mom and Shelley arrived minutes later, and I expected them to be distraught, but to my surprise they weren't. I'm sure it was because they were feeding off of my energy, and I was on a high. It was a type of ecstasy, and I think it was because I was feeling Danny's ecstasy at being freed from his body.

I wondered why I wasn't paralyzed with grief, why I was able to laugh and talk and enjoy my family and have the presence of mind to organize

Danny's memorial service and to finalize a slide presentation I'd been preparing about his life to show at the memorial. Shouldn't I be disconsolate and disheveled, unable to function? My face should have been red and swollen from crying, but I hadn't actually cried that much, and when I looked in the mirror I was shocked at how good I looked. Tired, yes, but I'd been looking tired for a long time. My face actually looked calmer than I'd seen it in years. Was this normal? Was I in denial? What *should* I have been feeling? Elishevaa had said that my grieving process would not be "normal." Is this what they meant?

During the years of Danny's disability I often described our relationship as being like the relationship between E.T. and Elliott from the movie "E.T." Elliott and his beloved E.T. were telepathically connected, feeling the same feelings and sharing the same thoughts, but eventually they had to separate. Danny and I were connected like that, but we never separated, and we most certainly are not separated now. I knew in my heart and in every cell of my body that I was *not* in denial, that I was not irrational or crazy with grief. I knew that Danny was with me and that he would guide me through this.

The next few days were typical of what people do when someone dies, though I can't say for sure because Danny was the first person close to me who'd ever died. My mother said that we should not hesitate to remove his clothes and belongings from his room, because the longer we waited the harder it would be to face. I agreed, and the process of going through his things, separating them into different boxes for Goodwill, for friends, etc., was not as painful as I'd imagined it would be. I felt he was standing right next to me the whole time, choosing which items would go where. Now and then a particular item would trigger a flood of tears, but it was cleansing, and an important part of the process. The pain was not an all-consuming, rip-out-your guts sort of pain. It was more like a gentle remembering, a wound in my heart that would open for a few minutes, fill with emotion and then seal up again. It was not what I expected. It almost felt *good*. It felt like *love*. Touching Dan's belongings and sharing their stories with Shelly, Jack and my mom was a very healing activity. In some ways I was numb, but in other ways I had never been more open in my life.

The first thing we did was to remove all the medical supplies from his room to clear the space of anything that suggested illness. I knew I'd be spending a lot of time in there, sleeping, meditating, dreaming and praying, and I wanted to make it a powerful, energized environment where health and balance could be found. His wheelchair went into the garage, and the diapers, waterproof bed pads, catheters, bath chair and other supplies were

15

divided between the local clinic and Dan's classroom where there were plenty of special needs kids who could use them.

Looking at these items from a distance made me realize just how dysfunctional Danny's body had become. It had been years since he'd been able to speak, feed himself or control his bowels and bladder. The catheters were a recent addition to his care arsenal since he'd lost the ability to urinate on his own. Catheterizing him three times a day, giving him an enema three times a week, bathing him every other day and spending at least an hour feeding him each of his meals was my entire life. So was singing to him, reading to him, watching movies with him, making him laugh, taking him for walks and loving him more than I'd ever loved anyone before, or ever will again. The years I'd spent as his mother were precious, as they would be for any mother. But the years I'd spent as a caregiver were *holy*.

I divided up his special possessions, keeping some for myself (I wear his socks and t-shirts to this day) and put various toys, trinkets and treasures aside for his friends. I gave my mother the dreamcatcher which hung on the wall above Danny's bed since he was a baby, and gave Amy the dog tags Danny was given by the fighter pilots at the Pt. Mugu Navy base on the day he was their special guest and they let him sit in the cockpit of an F-14.

Dan's model airplanes and framed pictures of airplanes went to Jack, because Jack had introduced him to the love of aircraft, and the two of them spent many hours together watching movies about World War II and playing a Playstation game called *Medal of Honor,* which never failed to whip Danny into a frenzy of laughter and excitement. Danny played the game when he still had motor skills and could use his hands, but even after he lost that ability, he loved to watch others play. Many of our friends delighted in this activity with Danny, and for a few years it was common to find a gaggle of guys in our living room playing Medal of Honor while Danny beamed in his wheelchair, laughing, kicking up his legs and giving his famous "thumbs up" sign (which he learned from the pilots at the Navy base).

As we were rifling through Dan's closet and drawers, we sniffed various items of clothing searching for anything that carried his scent. A characteristic of his illness was that he didn't perspire much, so he never really had any body odor, and yet we were surprised to discover that nothing we examined had any scent at all. Even the sheets where he'd slept and died had no particular smell to them, so we made it our mission to find something that smelled like Danny. The whole scene was quite funny, and we laughed as we inhaled socks and shirts and the dirty laundry that had piled up over the last week, but nothing smelled like him. At one point, Jack, with his usual dry sense of humor, walked into Danny's room and said, "He died and left us without a scent." We fell apart with laughter, and the story about searching for his scent with Jack's comment as the punch line became part of the text of the memorial service, which provided much-needed comic relief.

The service two days later was a joyous celebration of his life, and as I'd hoped, Danny made a personal appearance in the playful way people often do from the other side.

He made his presence known the first time when he caused the slide show to glitch, even after five perfect rehearsals of it earlier that day.

Nicole was 30 minutes late for the service, and with 100 people sitting there waiting, I couldn't delay things any longer, so we started without her. Everything went well until it was time for the slide show. For no apparent reason the laptop stopped communicating with the projector, and despite all attempts to re-link it, the system refused to work. In the middle of this, Nicole finally showed up, and the moment she sat down in her chair the system started up again. When the slide presentation was over, Lee Green stood up and pointed out to the assembly that Danny clearly did not want the show to start until Nicole arrived. The odd and wonderful thing about this was that I'd been working on this slide show for three years and had shown it to several people as the work progressed. I assumed that I'd shown it to Nicole somewhere along the way, but she told me later that she'd never seen it until that day. Danny obviously knew this.

Danny made his second appearance at the memorial service when Nicole was at the podium reading a beautiful little dedication she'd written for him. About halfway into her talk she paused, with a pained expression on her face, and said, "Eeeewww... there's a spider crawling on my paper." Everyone chuckled as I went up there to get rid of the spider. She continued her reading, and when she was finished, after hugging her and thanking her, I said to the crowd, "Danny sent that spider because he's having great fun acting like a normal big brother, and what's more normal than scaring your little sister with a spider?"

The audience roared with laughter, and later, a friend of mine who does maintenance for the building told me that in the two years he'd worked there, he'd never seen a spider in the place.

It was beautiful. Everything was beautiful, even the sadness. It was a potent, powerful time, and although there was constant hurting in my heart, it wasn't raw and harsh and suffocating like I'd expected to be. It was gentle, and flowed through me like stardust. I was in a daze most of the time and assumed I was simply numb. I remember telling someone that I felt as if I'd been abducted by aliens who'd done modifications to my mind and then put me back into my life, never to be the same again.

THE EGG AND THE ASHES

Funeral homes are altars to the fear of death. They reverberate with sorrow and a sense of smallness before a God who, like a sadistic puppeteer, can do impossible things like make us die "before our time." I now know that we not only have a say in when and how we die, we create every detail of our own lives and our own deaths, with God radiating in and around us as a power source to help us manifest those creations.

But funeral homes are not designed to acknowledge the love and light that is death. Most of them look like sets from 1950s horror movies, furnished with stuffy antiques, fake flowers, no windows and old men wearing outdated suits who look like corpses themselves.

While we were there arranging for Danny's cremation I had the idea for a franchise of New Age funeral homes. The walls would be painted in vibrant colors, and large windows would look out onto wild, beautiful gardens. This idea will make a mint when the time comes for the baby boom generation to make a mass exit.

Danny's ashes were delivered the day before the memorial service in an ugly plastic box, and that night Shelley, mom and I engaged in an unusual ritual. We'd purchased dozens of tiny plastic bottles with cork stoppers, some shiny gold fabric to wrap them in, and lengths of purple cord to tie around the bottle necks. These were used to hold small portions of ashes, and would be given as keepsakes to those who were closest to Danny. That was the original plan, but as we sat at the dining room table cutting squares of fabric and filling the bottles with the coarse sand that had once been my son's bones, Shelley had an idea.

"How would you feel if Warren and I took one of these on our motorcycle trip to the Colorado Rockies next month?" she asked. "We could sprinkle the ashes at Independence Pass and Danny could finally get to ride on a Harley!"

I could see Danny clapping his hands with glee and giving us a big thumbs-up. Shelly and her husband Warren were bikers, and road trips were their passion, and thus the "Danny World Tour' was launched. In the months that followed, dozens of friends carried the little bottles to the far corners of the world, honored to take them along on their vacations and business trips. So far Dan's ashes have been spread in the Rocky Mountains, Germany, the Grand Canyon, Italy, Puerto Rico, Las Vegas, Ireland, Austria and on a Caribbean cruise. He even tagged along with Amy's boyfriend Mark when he was deployed to Iraq. We all prayed that Danny's energy might help put an end to the war.

Three days after Danny died I took my first walk on the beach as a *former* caregiver, completely alone for the first time in years, no longer tethered to Danny's body. As I walked through the woods toward the deserted beach that had become my regular jogging route, Danny was instantly with me. He had a huge blown up body like a Macy's parade balloon, and he was in front of me and all around me. I laughed at this and said out loud, "I feel you, I really do! Is this real?" I was so excited, and felt indescribably happy. And I heard him say, "Yes, it's real."

I asked, "Will you stay with me, or will I lose you?"

And he repeated, "You'll always be able to access me easily when you can quiet the noise in your psyche. The work you've done in recent years, your meditations and spiritual practices, have been preparing you for this."

When I got to the beach the water was like glass, and I'd never seen it like that before. Danny was still with me and we began a conversation. I started by asking him to send healing energy to certain people, including Jack and Nicole, my mom and some others. And he assured me he would watch over them.

Then I told him that on the morning before he died I'd wanted to decrease his Morphine so that he'd be more alert and I could talk to him (and I instantly realized that I could talk to him now better than I could in years). He said to me, not really in words, but more in the form of complete thoughts placed inside my mind:

"I wasn't really there during those hours. I was barely attached to that body, and I was experiencing the most beautiful sensation of release. Nothing could have pulled me back, not the sound of the vacuum or the phone ringing or even your voice. I was like a baby bird coming out of an egg, but I didn't have to crack the egg, it opened itself, very slowly, and it let larger and larger amounts of light in, and I just floated up out of the egg, and there were people helping to lift me up. I was aware of the earth world, of you, and the house and everything around me, but it was very far off in the distance, and I wasn't paying any attention to it. All I cared about was being gently pulled out of this egg, because the feeling was so beautiful and

19

relaxing. The last time you saw me breathe I was held to the egg by the tiniest membrane, and finally I was free."

I sobbed with joy at hearing this, standing alone on the beach, just sobbing, so grateful to have connected with him and never wanting this moment to end. I found a stick and drew an image in the sand of an egg, open at the top, with Danny's perfect, precious soul floating out of it. After I drew the picture I walked further down the beach, and after a while turned back toward the sand picture.

As I approached the spot I felt a surge in my heart, something that might have been perceived as pain, but it wasn't. It was an opening. It felt like love. I've had plenty of broken hearts in my life and I know what they feel like, but this was something completely different. I cried and cried and said out loud, "This doesn't hurt! This feels amazing. What is this?" I thought maybe I was having a heart attack or something, but it didn't actually hurt, and then I realized that it felt good, really, really good, and I got an image of Danny putting his hands into my body and holding my heart in his hands and healing it. And just as I had that thought I heard him say:

"All the great teachers have been here to remind us of one thing... that we are not these bodies. Every death reminds us of this, and that's what grief really is. It's about remembering our spiritual home, our source, which some call "God." This source is the true definition of Heaven; it is the frequency on which we all operate, but we have lost sight of it. The pain of grief resonates on that same frequency because it's from the heart, and it's the same frequency as love. The pain of grief reminds you of home, just like love does when the heart opens. So in grief we cry and feel the frequency, and we want to be connected to the love we share with the person who has died, but in truth, we are just homesick for Heaven."

And as I stood there crying and thanking God and the guides and the angels for helping make this connection possible, I took the stick and wrote in the sand, "Thank you Danny."

2. Magical Night

Your loved ones on the other side, and even God itself, have no preferences about what you do with your life. They only want you to honor your soul's intention, and to know that you are both the creator and the creation.

Danny, from Heaven

During the last 18 months of Danny's life we lived in a small town called Odin (population 12,000), a resort community on Alabama's Gulf coast. Despite the classic southern stereotypes, Odin is an anomaly in the deep south; an extraordinary place which I've heard described as "a haven of aesthetics and progressive thinking on the Redneck Riviera."

The town was founded by radical tax evaders at the turn of the century, and has since been home to freethinkers, socialists, spiritualists, artists and others not typically found in small Alabama towns. Odin clings fiercely to its radical roots and is often referred to as "the island of Odin" because it's so different from the rest of Alabama. Odin has endless art and music festivals, street fairs, Earth Day celebrations, coastal clean-up campaigns and other creative activities, and my favorite of these was the First Friday Art Walk. On First Friday the shops serve refreshments, art is exhibited along the sidewalks and musicians play on every street corner. People stroll around drinking wine, visiting with friends and dancing in the streets. It's Odin at its finest.

We lived in Odin for more than a year before I finally got around to attending First Friday, and on July 9th, the night before Danny's 16th birthday, I packed him and his wheelchair into my van and drove downtown to join the party.

The day had started out badly and I was full of despair after weeks of non-stop fighting with Jack. As always, the same tired old internal dialog raged in my mind... *Why do I stay in this marriage? Maybe I should leave and rent a little house for Danny and me so that we can live in peace until he dies. No, it would be wrong to take him away from his home, he's comfortable there, and that's where he should die. But I'm so distraught all the time; I'm sure Danny can feel it. This is so unfair to him! God, I'm a terrible mother! How could I have subjected Danny to this kind of stress? What's wrong with me? Will he ever forgive me?*

Danny had just been released from the hospital after a battle with pneumonia, and I was overwhelmed, exhausted and bracing myself for what lay ahead. But the experience Danny and I had at First Friday made all my worries drop away and reminded me that there's a wonderful world out there full of joy, creativity and vibrant, loving human beings. Showing me this was one of Danny's many gifts to me during the last months of his life.

The streets of downtown Odin were alive with music, joy and community. We couldn't walk ten steps down the sidewalk without seeing someone we knew, including people I'd never met before who knew Danny from school or the clinic. Every five minutes someone came up to say hello, and they were so loving, like angels sent to remind me that we're all on the same frequency of love. Danny was like a guiding light that led me toward recognition of that love in ways I could never have imagined.

And what a light he was that night! At one point we sat down to listen to a duo playing Celtic music (my favorite), and a woman in her 70s came up to Danny, took his hand, and started dancing with him in his wheelchair while he laughed and kicked his legs. She turned out to be a retired special education teacher (teachers and nurses are always attracted to Danny when they see him in public). A little while later two more old ladies came up and did the same thing, taking Danny's hand and dancing with him, leaving him with red lipstick kisses all over his cheeks. After that we strolled down the street to a place called Andrew's, which by day is a gourmet deli but at night turns into a nightclub with live jazz and candles on the tables.

Danny was radiantly beautiful, sitting up straight and tall in his wheelchair, absorbing everything around him and listening to the music. I ordered a glass of wine for myself and some blueberry cream pie for Danny, and it felt like a very grown up thing to do, taking Danny to a place like this on the eve of his 16th birthday. He was my dream date, and as I sat there lovingly feeding him forkfuls of pie, I thought that even though he'd been in diapers since age nine and was unable to speak or feed himself, he was very much a man that night. I knew this beautiful evening would be one of our last special times together, and I wanted him to know that I understood he would soon be leaving and that he should not worry about me.

I wheeled his chair around so that he was directly facing me, and I leaned forward onto his lap with his hands in mine and said, "Look at my eyes Danny, and see how happy I am right now. I can see a great peace coming for both of us, and I want you to know that you never, ever, have to worry about me. Tonight I see that there's a whole new world out there, and I know I'll be happy in that world, even if you're not in it with me."

He looked at me with heart-melting love, with his medication-dilated pupils and blueberry cream dribbling out of his mouth, and smiled hugely, his eyes sparkling, and I knew he understood.

A WALK THROUGH HEAVEN

That night was like a walk through Heaven, dancing with members of our soul family, and I know we had this experience for a reason. At the time I thought it was because I'd been so despondent earlier in the day and needed to see that joy was possible, but I've since learned that this experience was intended to feel like a walk through *actual* Heaven, as Danny has now shown me from the other side. From that day on I was much more at peace and ready for the changes to come. I got Danny started with hospice care the following week.

Over the next few weeks Danny's body became less able to process food and he began losing weight rapidly. He was already skinny as a rail... in the *third percentile* of normal body weight for his age, with no fat reserves to live on. This was the anticipated course of the disease and we knew it was coming, but despite the fact that this had happened before and he'd eventually returned to his normal eating habits, I knew it would be different this time.

I dedicated myself to spending as much time with him as I could and to keeping our home environment as serene as possible. At night I'd lay by his side singing to him and gently telling him that that he could go back to Jupiter now, and that I would be OK here without him and would see him very soon. I told him that in Heaven -- or on Jupiter, or wherever he chose to go -- he could have any kind of body he wanted, and he could surf or ride a skateboard or fly without an airplane, and he could visit me anytime and neither of us would be lonely because our souls would still be together. I explained how there was no such thing as linear time on the other side, and that people can be in more than one place at the same time. I told him everything I knew, everything I'd learned in my metaphysical studies,

23

hoping he'd understand and wouldn't be afraid of dying. Of course he understood. He knew this stuff way better than I did.

I'd always believed that Danny was an advanced being, evidenced by the fact that he chose the body he did so that his life could be a tool for teaching unconditional love. I also knew that he chose the war zone of my marriage in which to carry out his soul's plan for growth. But it wasn't until Danny began to speak with me from the other side that I began to see the impact our family life had on this sweet, helpless boy who could do nothing but sit there silently observing the turmoil around him and absorbing all that disruptive energy. In these conversations he directed my attention to specific incidents from the last eight weeks of his life, a period in which he was drifting between two worlds and could see both of them clearly.

GUILT AND FORGIVENESS

One event we revisited immobilized me with guilt and shame, but also gifted me with profound insights. Danny was on heavy medication for muscle spasms, and the medication sedated him and suppressed many of his emotional responses. The drugs, combined with his neurological oddities, made him numb in many ways, and he was rarely able to express emotion or cry. During his last few months I'd decreased the meds a bit, which resulted in his becoming slightly more alert. I'd even heard of cases where lowering these doses actually made it possible for speech to return.

While feeding Danny one morning, Jack came into the kitchen and we began bickering about some inconsequential household issue. As was our usual pattern, the argument escalated out of control in 30 seconds. True to form, Jack shouted, "Why don't you just get the hell out of here already, bitch! I should just put you out on the street where you belong," and he stomped out of the room and headed down the hall. I volleyed back at him, "Nice going Jack. Nice thing to say in front of Danny. Don't worry, we'll both be out of here soon enough."

I was shaking and sobbing when I turned back to Danny, and to my astonishment, he was *crying,* and I hadn't seen him cry in three years. His face was scrunched up and his mouth was open and he was making a sort of wailing sound, and he looked at me with heartbreak and anguish in his eyes. I put my arms around him and said over and over again, "I'm sorry, I'm so sorry, I'm so sorry." The memory of his face at that moment will torment me forever.

24

This scene in itself was not unusual. Jack and I had screaming matches like this several times a week, and Danny was usually there to witness them. But this time Danny was crying, which was extremely rare for him. I realized at that moment that I'd been deluding myself by thinking that he was a little Buddha, above earthly concerns and impervious to human angst, and that these scenes didn't hurt him. I realized how the vicious verbal assaults, the threats of divorce, the dozens of times I'd fled in the night -- with Danny -- to a friend's house or a motel room, and all the times he'd seen me crushed and crying, must have shaken his sense of security and terrified him.

Although Danny was certainly advanced in his evolution, he was also a vulnerable, sensitive child, even more vulnerable because he was so dependent on me and unable to protect himself from physical or emotional harm. Normal children could have gotten up and left the house, or shouted out in protest when they saw their parents fight like that. Normal kids would have gone into their bedrooms and listened to loud music rather than listen to their parents arguing. Normal kids might have taken drugs or cut themselves or expressed their pain in any number of ways. They could run away. They could confide in their friends or ask another adult for help. But Danny could do *nothing*. Not even speak.

I was racked with guilt about this and probably always will be, even though when I was finally able to speak with Danny from Heaven, he not only put my mind at ease, he put the whole story in a higher spiritual context.

As he often does in these conversations, he gently steered the discussion away from the realm of the personal and into the realm of the universal. We had the following dialog a month after he passed, and it was in many ways more than I'd bargained for, but the lessons were worth their weight in gold:

ME: Tell me about the day Jack and I were arguing in the kitchen and you cried.

DAN: I cried not just for your pain but for Jack's too, because both of you were forgetting what you really are ... luminous souls doing your work on earth. You were forgetting Heaven, and I cried because I felt sad for your loss. I could see Heaven at that time, and it hurt me that you couldn't see it too. You don't need to apologize, and I don't need to forgive you, because you haven't done anything to me. You simply acted out the role we all agreed to before we came to earth.

25

The most important thing you saw that day was a reflection of your own belief system about relationships. The expression on my face was one of shock, which was the reaction of an emotionally healthy person. Jack's attack was unexpected, out of context and irrational, and would have horrified a person with healthy self-esteem, because such a person doesn't expect cruelty. But you've become numb and you don't even react to this type of injury any more. You *expect* it, and you've come to accept it as a normal part of your life. Your heart was hard, but mine was soft, and I wanted to show you what a soft, open heart looks like.

ME: This reminds me of something I read in a Sylvia Browne book. She said, "How can you teach a child to value respect and dignity while living in a house where these values don't exist?" And I wonder now Danny, you endured so many things that were a challenge to your dignity, like diapers, the wheelchair and being fed, yet you seemed to be at peace with that. But at the same time you were watching me voluntarily relinquish *my* dignity in this marriage. I can't imagine how that made you feel. There were very few examples of respect and dignity around you. I was supposed to teach that to you, and I failed.

DAN: Actually mom, I was supposed to teach that lesson to you. I challenged myself with the most undignified body one could have so I could focus on the dignity of the soul and expose you and Jack to that idea. We shared a common loss of dignity in a way, and now we're sharing a common healing. You and Jack were perfect partners for creating scenarios that would bring forth lessons about dignity and self-respect. You stayed with him for so long because you didn't believe you could take care of me on your own. But it turned out that you did the caregiving on your own anyway. Jack helped you in a very different way, by causing you to face your own issues about self-respect and dignity, which you've carried with you for many lifetimes. My helpless body was a glue to keep you with Jack until you learned those lessons.

ME: I'm so sorry Danny. I was so stupid. Will you forgive me? How will I know when I've learned those lessons?

DAN: You'll know because things will start to change. Either the relationship will transform or it will "end." You'll begin to release the attachment you have to the pain you've experienced with Jack, and you'll start to see him as a teacher. This will represent an enormous increase in your self-awareness, and when awareness increases, everything shifts, nothing can stay the same. Whether the relationship continues in its current form, whether you're physically together or not, is irrelevant, because relationships never really end, their form and structure simply changes.

In terms of me forgiving you, it's not necessary, nor is it possible, because it's not possible for me to judge you. We're made of the same energy; we're all one thing, one organism, not separate from each other or from God. So there can be no victim and no perpetrator. We are not separate enough to stand back and judge one another. If you want to say you're sorry, say it to yourself, and then release the guilt. Forgive yourself for closing your heart and forgetting what you are. The only sin that exists, the only pain that exists, is in forgetting your own divinity. I cried that day to show you this. I died to show you this as well.

ME: You died to show me this? That sounds like the idea of Jesus dying "for our sins."

DAN: Yes, that's right. It's exactly the same idea. Jesus came here as an *intervention*... to remind everybody that they'd missed the point about all being ONE. He died for our "sin" of forgetting our divine connection to love. The religion created by humans at that time was about taking power away from people and making them afraid of divine energy. Jesus dropped in to set the record straight, to remind us that we are more than just these bodies.

I began meditating daily, sometimes two or three times each day, and in the process Danny's voice became clearer and our encounters became more visual. In addition to images of himself, he'd show me landscapes, people, buildings, cities and symbols, much of which is explained in chapter six.

During one of these visual meditations I saw Danny in a place that looked like a vineyard with a beautiful little stone cottage and people working in the fields. This place was bathed in golden light and pulsed with energy. One of the men from the fields came forward to meet me and I later learned his name was "Arlen." He is a special teacher to Danny and an important member of our soul family who's been with Danny and me in other incarnations, usually in the role of teacher and guide. As I progressed in my ability to communicate with Danny, Arlen would regularly join in on our conversations.

Although I could hear and speak with Danny better than I could when he was alive, I missed his sweet little body terribly. On the one-month anniversary of his death, at roughly the same time he died, I laid on his bed to meditate. I wanted to put myself into the space that he was in during his last few hours, trying to feel what the separation from his body might have felt like, and trying to experience how he might have perceived the environment around him at the time.

I asked him to show this to me, and he gave me a clear picture of the difference between our bodies and our souls:

"Our bodies are like the little bottles you poured my ashes into. If the bottles represent the bodies, then the ashes contained within them represent the soul. The soul is part of the whole, part of the source, Heaven, God, creator, universal light, divine energy, whatever you choose to call it. When we incarnate, our essences are poured into our bodies, like the ashes were poured into the bottles. While I was dying, I was aware of the bodies around me, but they were just forms that contained essences. I was connecting more to the essences than to the forms, which is why I couldn't be pulled back to earth by the sound of your voice or the phone ringing. Even though your body was in the room, your energy, your soul -- the *real* you -- was all around me and I was relating to you on that level. The forms didn't matter."

I loved it when Danny talked to me of such things, but I also feared that he would just hang around for a short time to help me over the initial shock of his death and then leave me. So in most of our conversations, at least in the beginning, I'd ask him for reassurance. I'd also seek reassurance via readings with Rebecca and also with another medium I'd come to trust, Scott Christiansen. In one reading Scott said:

Your communication with Danny will go in cycles. Right now he's trying to catch up on things he's wanted to talk about for years, which is why it sometimes goes too fast for you. He'll give you things to think about and to process, and then he'll back off a bit and give you time to digest it, like a teacher giving an assignment and then leaving the student alone to do the work. He tends to check out when negative energy is present, just like he did when he'd witness the blow-ups with your husband. Danny was very sensitive and didn't want to be there at those times. He still does this from the other side by backing off when you're lost in fear or pain, because that energy repels him, and loving energy attracts him. It's a good incentive for staying in touch with him because it helps you release that stuff. His communications will get clearer as time goes on.

That information turned out to be completely true. Whenever I was obsessing about my marital issues or my life in general, Danny would not come in clearly. I quickly learned to burn off the anger by running on the beach and venting for five or ten minutes, and then consciously deciding that I was finished and ready to channel.

It worked every time.

3. A Family Memoir

"The souls in every family choose one another equally, and the experiences they share are magnificent, perfect manifestations of the plan made by each soul for its growth. With each experience, everybody has a chance to transform habits, responses, behaviors, beliefs and energy patterns. This is how family groups are supposed to function, which is why there can be no such thing as a dysfunctional family"

Danny, from the other side

The messages I receive from Danny are usually sparkling clear, but one message in particular surprised the heck out of me. Over a period of several weeks I got very strong impressions that he wanted me to use vignettes from my marriage to illustrate some of the teachings that would be shared in this book. I resisted this idea at first because I'd envisioned a book full of dazzling, esoteric cosmic truths, not a forum for whining about pathetic little human relationships. I also didn't want to wallow in my own personal drama or whimper about what a tough life I had, so I had plenty of reasons to question this plan.

But Danny was insistent, and I soon learned that the content of this book is really out of my hands. My job is to simply provide structure and narrative while taking dictation from Danny and the other guides who've signed on to this project. Danny teaches, as do others, that we create the exact scenarios we need in our earth lives in order to propel our souls forward in their insatiable quest for growth and experience. Using my family dynamics to illustrate this point began to make sense as the book unfolded and the teachings came through. I've since learned not to question this guidance. I'm working with a team of discarnate editors and co-writers, and they can be uncompromising. So here, with apologies for anything that hints of self-indulgence or victimhood, is my spiritual family memoir.

THE BEGINNING

It's actually more painful to write about my marriage and family life than to write about Danny's physical suffering and death. The true face of my marriage was covered in darkness and denial, and I realize now that I kept it that way in the name of creating a stable life for Danny. I'm amazed at how much I lied to myself about this.

Danny was a normal, healthy boy until the onset of his illness at age seven, and as if on cue, he began to show symptoms just a few weeks after Jack, the man who would become Danny's stepfather, entered our lives. I understand now that this was a soul contract created by the three of us before we came into this incarnation. When Jack showed up it was as if Danny looked at him and said, "Good, you've arrived. Now we can get this party started."

Clichés like "stormy" or "dysfunctional" are pitifully inadequate to describe my relationship with Jack. It toggled between emotional ferocity and detached hostility, was physically violent on occasion, and distinguished the rest of the time by fearful withdrawal and icy contempt on my part, manipulation and verbal abuse on his. During our nearly 10 years together we split up six times.

When Danny's illness first presented in the form of cognitive and behavior problems, his teachers at school thought he might be depressed or have learning disabilities. His father Jim and I had divorced amicably when Danny was four, and we got along beautifully as former spouses. The first few years after the divorce Jim lived a mile away and kept Danny with him on alternating weeks, and the two of them were closer to each other in this configuration than they'd been when we lived together as a family.

After the divorce I had a three-year relationship with Michael, a business associate I'd known for more than a decade who showed up at my office one day and swept me off my feet. Danny adored him, and Michael blended easily into our life. We were the hub of an extended family that included Jim and whomever he was dating at the moment, along with assorted relatives and friends who comfortably got together with us for holidays, birthday parties and other celebrations.

Those were good years, but the relationship with Michael eventually ended and it was hard for Danny to see him go. I suppose Danny had good reason to be depressed, but the source of his problems turned out to be something much more insidious. Not long after Michael left the picture, Jack stepped in. He'd moved to Los Angeles on the promise of a Hollywood screenwriting career, having left his wife and five year-old daughter Nicole back in Florida. His divorce was a messy one, with Nicole firmly installed as a pawn in the middle. Our attraction was intense and immediate.

He was movie star handsome, super smart, and the sex was phenomenal. I was a goner from day one, hopelessly smitten by this beautiful, intelligent man, and eight months after we met, Jack moved in with Danny and me. But after only a few weeks, the sensitive, articulate Romeo I fell in love with mysteriously disappeared and was replaced by a brooding, irrational stranger who alternated between erratic bouts of anger and long periods of stony wordlessness.

There was a small guest house out back, which Jack had set up as his office, and it quickly became the place where he'd retreat when any sort of conflict arose between us. I was experienced enough at relationships to understand a man's need for his "cave," and I'd learned to respect Jack's requirement for a lot of space. But I never could have imagined that he'd sequester himself in that room and refuse to speak to me for days at a time. I learned to flow with his rhythm, believing that after he'd had time to mull things over he'd come out and we could begin a dialog with the intention of resolving the problem. But it never happened that way.

Instead, when he'd finally emerge, he'd act as if nothing had happened. When I'd ask, "Can we talk about this?" He'd reply blankly, "Talk about what?" and then go about his day seeming to have no recollection of previous events. If I tried to initiate a discussion he'd get angry and return to his office for another day or two, almost as if he were punishing me for intruding on his silent world. And it worked. I soon learned that if I didn't rock the boat by trying to talk about things, we'd maintain a state that somewhat resembled peace.

But if anything did manage to scratch the surface of his protective layer, he'd lash out viciously and then crawl back into his shell. When it came to communication we were oil and water. During our first year together, Jack's daughter Nicole, who was the same age as Danny (seven at the time), came to visit for Christmas and again for a few weeks in the summer. Jack's divorce from Nicole's mother was a hotbed of conflict, and these visits were punctuated by telephone arguments and angry faxes exchanged between them almost daily. Nicole was confused about her dad's new living situation, and despite our feeble attempts at blending our new little family, everything was a struggle and issues were rarely resolved.

Jack criticized my house, my dog, my political views, my work, my friendships, my education and my parenting skills, yet all the while told me I was the most interesting, intelligent, beautiful woman he'd ever known and that he was head-over-heels in love with me. But he spent most of his time in the guest house/office, and when we did spend time together, his mood was unpredictable, turning on a dime between affection and shutting me out with no explanation. His Jekyll and Hyde behavior kept me fearful and vigilant 24 hours a day, and I blamed myself for everything, twisting myself into knots trying to please him. I figured if I lowered my expectations and tried to be sweeter, sexier and more accommodating, with fewer needs and more patience, we would be happy. At least that's what Jack kept telling me.

But nothing worked, especially anything that might require conversation. If I tried to work through a simple problem with him, he'd tell me I was blowing things out of proportion and then go into his office and lock the door, only coming out to use the bathroom or get something to eat. During his brief sojourns into the main house I'd apologize for whatever I'd done to upset him (I had no idea what I was apologizing for), but no matter what I said, he'd remain silent, and if I tried to break through the silence, he'd lash out viciously. Sometimes while he was locked in his office I'd go out there and beg him, through the closed door, to talk to me. But he'd act as if he didn't hear me. He was so silent and unresponsive that I sometimes wondered if he'd gone in there and had a heart attack or killed himself.

Once I got so frustrated after two solid days of the silent treatment that I hysterically banged on the door, demanding that he come out. There was no answer as usual, but a few seconds later he burst through the door, pinned me down on the ground and threatened to hit me if I continued to "harass" him. Nicole and Danny witnessed this exchange, the first of many like it over the years.

Maybe he was right. Maybe my insistence on open communication *was* a form of harassment and I should have just shrugged my shoulders and walked away when he was in one of his moods (eventually I learned to do that, but it took years). I spent the first three years of our relationship thinking there was something wrong with *me*, and Jack was more than happy to agree. He continually told me that I had a "defect in my personality" and that I needed therapy to manage my "anger problem." So I went to therapy, but I learned something that Jack could never have anticipated... that ignoring, blaming, withdrawing, name-calling and criticizing are forms of verbal abuse.

Meanwhile, Danny had begun to exhibit disturbing behaviors at school. I'd get calls almost daily because he was hitting kids, wetting his pants, having a hard time focusing in class and using bad language. The school psychologist assumed it was because of problems at home, and this was certainly a reasonable assumption. But nobody could have guessed that the cause of his symptoms would turn out to be a rare metabolic disorder that manifested in its early stages as cognitive and behavioral problems. The changes in Danny were slow and subtle, yet he remained a sweet, happy boy, gifted at reading and spelling, enjoying video games, Lego models and a large circle of friends. Life was good for Danny, despite the gathering storm around him.

Four months after moving in with us, Jack declared he was moving out. Things were rocky, but the relationship was only a year old and I was under the impression that we'd work to resolve our problems rather than giving up so easily. When I suggested counseling he refused, and he also refused to talk to me about his feelings or why he was leaving. I was devastated when he left, but six weeks later, as would become our pattern, we reunited. He told me he loved me and couldn't imagine life without me, but didn't like the "energy" in my house, didn't like my dog and didn't like being around Danny. So he proposed a plan. We would spend every *other* week together... the weeks that Danny was at Jim's.

He rented an apartment across town and for the next six months I led a double life as a mother one week, a lover the next. During the weeks that Danny was with me, Jack and I talked on the phone and emailed, but he would not come to my house, nor was I allowed to go to his, because he was busy during the day working with Barry, his screenwriting partner. It worked out so that we were only together when Danny was at Jim's. I felt like a traitor to my son, who needed me more than ever.

The week-on-week-off arrangement continued for six months until I broke down and told Jack how unhappy I was about splitting myself between him and Danny. The topic came up in the car while we were on our way to a ski resort for a press junket with a group of journalists (one of the many free "vacations" I received through my work as a travel writer). As usual, he got angry, refused to discuss it, and went into radio silence for the rest of the trip. At dinner that night with the journalists I put on a happy face while Jack sat there brooding. Back in our room he turned away from me in bed and would not speak to me at all. I cried most of the night, and a few times tried to hold him and apologize for upsetting him, but he lay there like a stone, unmoving and unresponsive. I finally got out of bed, got some blankets from the closet and slept on the floor. The next morning Jack demanded to be taken home and

I readily obliged, humiliated in front of my colleagues, who could clearly see that something was wrong.

We made the six-hour drive back to Los Angeles with me at the wheel and Jack in the passenger seat staring straight ahead in complete silence. About once each hour I'd try to speak to him, asking if he was OK and apologizing for whatever I'd done wrong, but my attempts to engage him only made him angrier and more firmly barricaded. When I dropped him off at his apartment he told me he never wanted to see me again. This was our second breakup, but three weeks later we were back together. This time he agreed to rebuild his relationship with Danny.

During this phase there were a few good times, especially when Nicole would visit and we'd hang out together as a family. But those times were rare, and Danny and I usually ended up alone because something would make Jack angry (I never knew what), and he'd leave me in tears, go back to his apartment and disappear for two or three days. If I called him, he'd hang up on me and then unplug his phone. I'd berate myself for upsetting him (though I was never sure what I'd done wrong) and discipline myself to leave him alone, keeping myself busy with friends and other activities until he'd finally call, and in his most cheerful voice, brimming with sweet talk, he'd chat casually as if nothing had happened. I'd go along with it and we'd pick up where we left off. The issue -- whatever it was -- would never be spoken of again.

He trained me well. I learned not to question him, not to ask him to explain his behaviors or express his feelings, and to keep my own feelings to myself, avoiding confrontation, tempering my honesty, denying my needs and giving him unlimited space. I realized years later that in my past relationships I'd put communication at the top of the list of qualities I valued in a partnership. But I remember consciously deciding to move it lower down on the list in order to be with Jack. If I broke any of his rules, he'd punish me by shutting me out, which played beautifully into my fear of abandonment. He knew exactly how to control me and keep me from penetrating his armor. The system was firmly in place.

In January of 2000 Danny was diagnosed with a rare disease called Metachromatic Leukodystrophy (MLD), which would slowly rob him of his ability to walk, talk or control any of his basic bodily functions. His life expectancy would be 5-10 years, and as he degenerated he would require total care. On the heels of this shattering news, Jack suggested that we move in together again and start living like a "real family." I was suspicious of his sudden interest in family life, which seemed so incongruous with his past behavior, and suggested that maybe it would best to end the relationship rather than to make new commitments that would bind him to a dying child. But he insisted that he wanted to go through this with me and that he wanted to be there for Danny, and I believed him.

In May we rented a big, beautiful house in Thousand Oaks, California, a quiet suburb about 30 miles north of Los Angeles. But the honeymoon was over before it began, because as we were moving in, Jack told me that he didn't want me to unpack anything, make any decorating decisions or even put toilet paper in the bathroom without his supervision. Two weeks later, on Mother's Day, we had a huge fight in which he told me that I had bad taste in furniture, no sense of style, and that I had the home decorating skills of a "nigger" (years later, when I became friends with his previous wife -- an artist with exquisite taste -- she told me that he'd said the exact same words to her). Stunned and bewildered, I took Danny and headed to my mother's for the weekend. She thought we were there to celebrate Mothers Day, but instead it was the first of many such escapes to my mother's, my sister's and sometimes even to a motel a mile away from the house.

THE MIDDLE

For the next two years I was the classic partner of an emotional abuser. I blamed myself for everything that went wrong, apologized for things I didn't do, wore down my friends with tearful late-night phone calls and was resolute that somehow, somewhere there would be a light at the end of the tunnel. I tried endlessly to understand why this intelligent, articulate man resorted to assailing my character and using malicious verbal barbs to fend off my attempts at normal conversation. I walked on eggshells all the time and began to doubt myself and to believe the vile things he said about me. The relationship kept me so emotionally drained that I felt myself shrinking to nothingness, dishonoring my values and questioning my sanity. I was so skilled at convincing myself that my need for communication and respect was "wrong" that I began to believe that I didn't really need those things in the first place. On the advice of another therapist I began keeping a journal, recording Jack's bizarre reactions and cruel words.

In our Thousand Oaks house Jack's office was in the corner of our large living room, and he required that the house stay quiet from 9 am to 6 pm because those were his work hours. That was easily manageable, because Danny left for school at 7:30 in the morning and was gone until 3:00. A state disability program paid for in-home child care after school, so Danny would come home around 3:00, and Jenny, his caregiver, would play with him in his room, take him to the park or give him a bath in the afternoons.

But Jack felt that Jenny and Danny's presence was disruptive, and insisted that Danny stay away from the house until exactly 6:00 each day. So I arranged for Jenny to keep Danny at her house for those three hours. After Jenny brought Danny back home at 6:00, we'd have dinner and then spend the evening in the family room adjacent to the kitchen, watching tv with the volume turned low so as not to disturb Jack, who would be working in the living room until late at night. Sometimes he wouldn't be working at all, but would watch tv in there while Danny and I watched the same show in the room next to the kitchen. Even though we lived together and attempted to act like a family, Jack kept his distance.

During the fourth year of the relationship, motivated by the progression of Danny's illness, lots of therapy and piles of self-help books, I started to wake up. With the help of counselors, angels and others, I started learning how to set boundaries and build self-esteem. I stopped apologizing and stopped trying to force communication. I found a group of parents in my community who had disabled children and they became my closest friends. I started an on-line support group for families all over the world who had children with MLD. I made sure Danny had everything he needed in terms of school, doctors, therapists, friends and other support systems, and spent every minute I could playing with him, loving him, reading to him, taking him on trips and just *being* with him. I loved Danny's sweet company, and turned my full attention to him, which is where it should have been all along. I still loved Jack and wanted an intimate relationship with him, but I no longer trusted him. I still tried to communicate and to resolve problems with him, but I didn't try as hard, and when he'd get angry and lock himself in the bedroom, I just let him stay there. I had more important things to worry about.

A year later Danny began to seriously decline. Somewhere along the way he stopped walking and his speech began to fail, but amazingly, he was still the sweetest, funniest, most affectionate kid you could ever imagine. Everyone who knew him -- friends, family, teachers, babysitters -- was madly in love with him. I nicknamed him "happycake" because he was truly the happiest boy in the world and a delight to be around. As he lost the ability to use words he would simply laugh instead. And he laughed all the time.

I had long since stopped trying to share my feelings with Jack, especially my concerns about Danny. My son would not live more than a few years, but I didn't dare show any emotion, because I knew my words would be either twisted or ignored by Jack, and that my feelings would be mocked, dismissed and ridiculed. Once, when I told him that keeping Danny out of the house until 6 pm every day was becoming a problem for both me and the sitter, the conversation disintegrated into an argument that ended with Jack saying, "Oh poor little you, everybody has to feel sorry for you because your kid's dying. Your life isn't any harder than any other mother's. Maybe your friends fall for it when you play the Danny card, but *I* don't."

Breakup number three came during our fifth year together, when Jack decided to move across the country while we were in the midst of shopping for a house and planning a wedding. He'd been enthusiastic about the wedding ceremony, helping with decorations and other details, although the wedding was to be ceremonial only, because a license would have meant a legal and financial entanglement that Jack didn't want, nor was he willing to wear a wedding ring. The invitations had already been mailed and we were about to make an offer on a house when he declared his intention to leave.

His announcement was preceded by a big blowup in which he'd twisted my arm using one of his karate moves and ended up fracturing my elbow. We were standing in the hallway arguing about who-knows-what, and I was pleading with him to sit down to talk with me about it. I reached for his hand and tried to lead him into the living room where we could sit and talk, but he twisted my hand to the outside in a wristlock that forced me to the ground. When I went to a doctor three days later because the pain in my arm had become unbearable, I told her I was a martial arts student and that the injury had occurred in my karate class.

A week later Jack drove off in a U-Haul truck headed for Florida, and two weeks after that he'd purchased a house for himself. Six weeks later, after a string of regretful phone calls and mushy emails, he came up with another plan... this time it was legal marriage, rings and all, and a long-distance relationship.

His proposal came via an eloquent, apologetic email followed by more mushy, marathon phone calls, and I accepted, but didn't tell my friends or family because I knew they'd try to talk me out of it. Jack flew in from

Florida and we took four friends with us to a bed & breakfast in the mountains (one of them was a minister), and had the ceremony in our suite. We sent an email to friends and family announcing our marriage *after* the deed was done.

My parents and friends were horrified that I would not only reunite with him, but actually marry him on these terms, but they supported me the best they could. It was clearly a plan designed to avoid a real relationship, but I was hopeful, because Jack had convinced me that he recognized the need for change, and promised he'd see a therapist. For the next two years we lived on opposite coasts, and he'd fly in to "live" with me for two weeks each month. Being self-employed and working with freelance clients via phone and email made this possible.

During Jack's visits we did nothing but fight, and when he was back home in Florida he'd complain bitterly to me by phone about his financial problems, his overgrown lawn and his lower back pain. When I'd offer help or advice (including offering to pay for a gardener to take care of the lawn), he'd tell me I was meddling and trying to control him. So I disciplined myself to simply listen without comment, which was not easy for me, being a problem solver by nature. When I'd manage to interject something, usually asking for clarification about a point he was making that I didn't understand, he'd accuse me of diverting and interrupting him. My questions were never answered and issues were never resolved.

About five months after we were married, he started telling me that I was "not committed enough to the marriage." I had no idea what he meant by this, since my focus and energy was so completely wrapped up in him that I was neglecting my own well being as well as Danny's. When I asked him to explain, he refused to discuss it further, and merely repeated the phrase, "You don't know the meaning of commitment" over and over again. I'd tearfully plead, "What have I done to make you think such a thing? What do you mean? I don't understand." But he'd simply re-state the same phrase with no explanation other than admonishing me to stop nagging him about it. I even arranged a phone consultation with a mediator in the hope that he could help us discuss this, but Jack skillfully avoided the mediator's questions and the conversation went nowhere. Eventually this issue, like all the others, just floated away, unexamined and unresolved.

The next two years resulted in two more breakups (initiated by me this time), and two more reconciliations. In our final reunion I agreed to move to Florida with Danny and our new dog, Jackson, in concurrence with Jack's insistence that the only chance for our marriage would be "if we were equally invested financially in a new life with a real home." Even Nicole responded to this idea and asked to come live with us, and to our surprise her mother agreed. The plan came together perfectly when we discovered a beautiful little town called Odin, Alabama, about 50 miles across the Florida border from Nicole's mom, and I found that I could easily set Danny up with the social, medical and school services he needed there (he was now in a wheelchair full-time, wearing diapers, and almost completely non-verbal). We bought a gorgeous 3400 square-foot house on a creek, and I had high hopes for our future.

But within four weeks the glimmer faded from our little fantasy, and things began to unravel. The challenge of an instant family that included a teenage daughter and a dying son required more focus and more communication than Jack could comfortably manage. A week after Danny and I arrived, Jack came down with the flu and was sick for three weeks, which didn't help his disposition. When he wasn't sleeping he spent his time yelling and snarling at Nicole and me. In the second month I had to face a life-or-death decision for Danny, which Jack refused to discuss with me while we waited in the emergency room. And in the fourth month the dog had to be put to sleep because he attacked Jack.

It was impossible to address even the simplest issues -- such as Nicole wanting to go out with her friends, or where to store the boxes of Christmas decorations -- without arguments that triggered violent rages in Jack and caused Nicole to hide out fearfully in her room. After the incident with the dog, Nicole moved back to her mom's and rarely felt safe around her father again.

Later that summer I had a T.I.A (Transient Ischemic Attack, also known as a "mini stroke"), and a few months after that I had a second one. Miraculously, I recovered with no permanent damage, but I was exhausted from Danny's care, which had become more of a full-time job as his illness progressed. More importantly, I was beaten down and demoralized by the constant turmoil with Jack. At one point I fantasized about committing suicide and taking Danny with me, and I read up on the correct drugs and dosages to do the job. But my guides intervened and showed me what a mistake that would be. So instead I vowed that I would not move Danny again, since he had grown comfortable with his life in Odin, but I would leave Jack for good after Danny died.

In Jack's defense I have no doubt that he loved Danny. He treated Danny with affection, and always came along to school meetings and clinic appointments. Jack played Medal of Honor with Danny regularly, and even made a special switch that Dan could hit with his fist to fire the guns (Danny was losing the use of his hands at this point). Jack also built models of the airplanes and showed them to Danny whenever they'd play the game, explaining the guns, the decals and other details. Sometimes he'd rent DVDs of old Star Trek and Kung Fu episodes and watch them with Danny, cracking jokes, singing silly songs and making the whole experience quite entertaining. The two of them did some serious male bonding this way, and Danny enjoyed the time they spent together. They were buddies in this sense, and I know Danny loved him.

Even though he bonded with Danny in his own way, Jack kept his distance in other ways. He wouldn't eat meals with us because he felt "too crowded at the table with the wheelchair there," so he'd eat standing at the kitchen counter while Danny and I sat at the table. When he was finished he'd put his dishes in the dishwasher and leave the room without a word. He'd help with Danny's care if I asked him to assist with a specific task, such as helping me carry Danny into the shower or sitting with Danny while I went out to run errands. If a diaper needed changing while I was out, Jack would do it, but the unspoken agreement was that Danny's care was my exclusive domain. He once told a therapist of ours that he saw his role as "comparable to a neighbor who lends a hand in an emergency." He said he didn't want to be *expected* to help with Danny, but would assist with specific tasks, if asked, on a case-by-case basis. He said that his time was his own and he had a right to use it as he chose, and if I wanted my life to be about taking care of a sick child, that was my choice, but it didn't mean that *he* had to spend *his* time that way. He also said that if I needed extra help I should just hire extra babysitters, because after all, isn't that what the child support from Jim is supposed to pay for?

I came to realize that Jack's relationship with Danny was more like an older sibling than a stepfather, which from my perspective made Jack seem more like a teenage son to me than a husband (which had a lot to do with my loss of sexual interest in him). Finally I became so uncomfortable with the idea of asking Jack for help that I simply stopped asking. I lifted and carried Danny by myself, and even took him along to the grocery store, pushing the wheelchair in front of me with one hand and pulling the grocery cart behind me with the other. Sometimes I'd unload Danny, his chair and the groceries all by myself while Jack sat on the couch watching TV. If I asked for help he'd comply, but f I didn't specifically ask, he'd stay engrossed in his tv show without even looking up as I walked past. I worried constantly that I would have another stroke.

It wasn't until after his death that I realized how frustrated and frightened Danny must have been all those years. He witnessed horrible scenes of name-calling, door slamming, furniture being broken and cars screeching away in the night, but being non-ambulatory and non-verbal, there was nothing he could do to express his discomfort. He couldn't speak, couldn't run away and couldn't even pull the bedcovers up over his head to hide from the scary monsters screaming at each other in the next room. So when I realized that he has something to say about all this *now,* I knew how important it was to include scenes from my marriage in this book. Here are some of Danny's comments about our family:

"As you face these painful memories and the many truths that are being revealed to you now, you begin the process of walking through a purifying fire, and you've chosen to take the bold path and not skip any steps. You're fiercely committed to this, and it's going to be painful at times. But for humans in physical life, pain is necessary to stimulate change. We can always choose to sidestep what we perceive as unbearable pain, for example, you can leave Jack and immediately find another relationship, or you can stay with Jack in an attempt to avoid the acute pain of releasing the old energies that your ego holds dear. But you're choosing to be done with these issues once and for all, and when that happens, your health and your life will be radiant.

I knew when I came in that I would not have physical means of expression, but I did have the skills of patience and listening and stillness. I brought with me the ability to operate on several frequencies at once, which is what makes it possible for us to speak to each other like we do now. When I felt the struggle between you and Jack I encased myself in a cocoon surrounded with light, and I turned myself into a reflecting device that sent love back toward the two of you. In doing that I was able to give more love to myself as well, because when you send love out, you charge it up from within, like stoking a fire. But that doesn't mean it didn't hurt to experience these things. My heart ached for both of you and I was very afraid at times. But now, from my perspective in Heaven, I understand how the words and actions of others are our own creations. They are tools for building bridges back to our sense of belonging with the divine.

In the months to come you will release your anger and carry no malice in your heart toward Jack at all. You will bless him and release him completely to his path. For now, do not engage, do not need to be heard or to be right, just let go with love. When you feel yourself getting caught up in fear or emotions, focus on ME. Look into my eyes the same way an emergency rescuer tells the person he's rescuing to look into his eyes to keep from panicking.

In every interaction you have with Jack, no matter what is being said or done, remember that you are of Heaven and the discord is not. This will keep you open and ventilated so that you can receive messages from your guides and from God. Like the Course in Miracles says, "I can see peace instead of this." There was a reason why that particular line stuck with you the way it did when you read that book. Think of nothing but this. Don't worry about the future. You will receive many signs about what to do next."

4. Song to the Higher Self

"To solve problems in human life, there is no other guidance and no other source of information than the Higher Self, which receives its messages directly from God, and God is an energy that burns and energizes us like a pilot light. If you want to receive the truth, ask from the Higher Self, not from the ego. For example, the ego asks, 'Should I stay in this marriage or should I leave?' But the Higher Self asks, 'Lead me to whatever best serves the truth and allows me to live according to my core values and to do what I came here to earth to do.'

Of course you're *already* doing what you came here to do, because you choose every thought and every action, and whatever you choose steers you along your path. But the path can always change because you have free will, and awareness always triggers change. As you gain each new piece of awareness, the whole game board transforms, people and places shift, and you make new decisions based on the new information you've received. That's how free will works.

Your awareness increases all the time, and with each degree of increase a thousand new possibilities are revealed. With this constant flow of awareness, it's impossible for you to stay in the same place you were before. You can make a million dollars or live in poverty, marry or divorce, or even kill yourself, it doesn't matter. Whatever you do, you're following the plan you created in Heaven, a plan designed to propel you to higher awareness. The lessons built into your plan will come to you one way or another. With increased awareness, you start to realize that you are actually creating situations that bring forth exactly the lessons you came here to address. Anything you miss or avoid you'll get later, so there's no hurry. You have all the time in the world, literally."

Danny, from the other side

On our first Christmas without Danny, 14 weeks after his death, we didn't decorate the house, buy gifts or get a tree, because the world had stopped. I'd made up my mind to leave, Danny and Nicole were both gone and our home was childless and joyless. I'd been trying for months to tell Jack that I'd reached a state of complete hopelessness about our marriage and that I was serious about divorce. I asked him once again if he'd return to counseling, and once again he refused. I tried to talk with him about the state of our union, approaching him as gently and gingerly as I could, looking for any shred of hope or spark of connection that might lead to a new idea for healing our relationship. But my attempts to engage him in conversation were routinely dismissed, demeaned or ignored, as they had been for the entire nine years of our life together. And I finally realized that I didn't need any more evidence that our communication dynamic was *not* going to change.

We'd been sleeping separately for seven months and had stopped going to counseling... on the advice of our counselor. She'd suggested that we quit working on our marriage temporarily to concentrate solely on dealing with Danny's death, and then, when we felt ready, we could come back and she would help us negotiate the next step. Jack had initially agreed to this plan, but when the time came to go back, he insisted that he'd never agreed to it in the first place. At that point it hardly mattered, because there was nothing left to negotiate.

By now I'd been conversing with Danny and Arlen regularly. They'd devised a sort of teaching hierarchy, each taking on a specialty area in which either or both could guide me. There were times when Danny made it very clear that he wouldn't answer questions about my future or my relationship with Jack, especially during this time of turmoil when I was planning to leave my marriage. This frustrated me at first, because after all, I was talking to *Heaven,* so couldn't I expect to get glimpses into the future? I was naive then, not well versed in the way divine guidance truly worked, but Danny and Arlen slowly taught me.

In the beginning when I'd pose questions to Danny about my marriage or my future plans, I'd either get nothing, or he would speak in loving words, supporting my efforts at growth but never giving specific information. I came to learn, with the help of other mediums like Scott and Rebecca, that Danny had a very specific role, as did Arlen. Whenever I was obsessing about the marriage (and boy, did I ever obsess, to the point where I started wearing a rubber band around my wrist so I could snap it every time I got too involved with blame or drama, thereby programming myself away from that behavior), Arlen would usually come through to offer guidance while Danny waited lovingly in the background. I knew that he and Arlen were not only guides, they were protectors. They always offered me the opportunity to choose a higher view of any situation and to take a higher path. But they also allowed me to follow my heart and use my free will, and never judged me for having human emotions. Nor did they -- or any guides -- ever tell me what I "should" do.

One night during my endless struggle over whether or not to leave Jack, and during a time when I was praying and meditating intensely every day, I had an amazing dream with a crystal clear message. It happened on a night when I'd decided to go back to Jack's bed after six months of sleeping separately. I don't know what I had in mind or what I expected, maybe it was a last-ditch attempt to connect and reconcile. But I think what it really was, spiritually speaking, was a way for me to put myself in a situation where this dream could come to me. *This* is how guidance from spirit truly works.

On that night I'd attempted once more to speak to Jack from my heart, taking great pains not to be critical or to blame, but to simply reveal that I was losing hope that our relationship could ever be healthy. Naturally he ignored me and left the room in the middle of the conversation, screaming that the only problem in our marriage was my "constant negativity." Being a caregiver by nature and being fearful of Jack's extreme reactions, I regretted stirring things up, so in the middle of the night I crawled into bed with him and snuggled up to him, trying to smooth things over, which meant, in essence, that I was trying to buy back my truth as I had done a thousand times over the years.

But within minutes of getting into the bed I immediately had trouble breathing, my heart started palpitating and I couldn't get comfortable. I also noticed sharp sciatic pain on my right side, which had troubled me for the past year or so but had subsided after Danny died. Now it returned with a vengeance. I was extremely agitated and there was no way I'd be able to sleep in this state, but I was determined to stay in that bed. After about 90 minutes I fell asleep and had this dream:

I was living in our old house in Thousand Oaks and Danny came back. I was carrying him in my arms, and put him into the recliner chair in the living room to watch tv while I began making some food for him and doing other caregiver tasks. I thought to myself, "Oh my God, this is beginning all over again; he's come back with the same disabled body, and it will be the same life we had before." Then I noticed there was a bed in the room next to where Danny sat, and suddenly Jack and I were in this bed. Jack was wanting to have sex with me, but I knew it was emotionally risky and I had no interest in it. And besides, Danny was in the room with us, and so was Nicole.

Then Danny got up and walked out of the room. I followed him to a back door of the house and he expressed to me (without words) that it was time for him to go back to Heaven. I was afraid I'd offended him by "complaining" about our old life starting over again, and thought maybe that's why he was leaving. But he didn't seem the least bit upset. He was smiling and laughing and had one of those electric scooters with him, and he hopped on it and rode it down the street just as a big semi truck came by. He intentionally crashed right into the wheels of the truck and died. But I knew it was OK, it was just a method he chose for getting back home to Heaven.

Then a mail carrier came to the front door and gave me a letter, which was a black & white photocopy of a greeting card that said, "Heal the pain of addiction." There was a hand-written note with the card saying that Danny had a special message for me, but I had to go to the morgue to pick it up. So I went to the morgue and there was the original of the greeting card, but this time it was in color, with the same message about addiction. There was some handwriting on the bottom, which was an additional message from Danny, but I woke up before I could read it.

Needless to say, this dream blew my mind. I knew immediately that the addiction Danny was referring to was the addictive patterns I'd fallen into with Jack (trying to force communication, focusing on his issues rather than my own, seeking his approval, validation, etc.). I also loved the symbolism of my thinking "this is beginning all over again," which had nothing to do with caregiving but everything to do with my having a choice about whether or not to fall back into old relationship patterns. And I love the part about Danny crashing into the truck. He didn't have a body, so it didn't matter. He could have jumped off a cliff or drowned in a bathtub or been eaten by Godzilla. Any of those things would have simply been transportation back to Heaven.

This dream seemed so important that I needed a second opinion, so of course I called Rebecca for a reading with Elishevaa, and they said:

Loved one, as you know, Danny does not normally want to get involved in what happens between you and Jack, for he wants you to process this yourself, as it is part of your growth. But if you listen carefully to your story, your giving Jack physical comfort was a result of guilt, which was a result of sharing your truth. Danny WILL have a tendency to become involved when you are so close to breaking an old pattern, and then begin to fall back into that pattern. As you've noticed, things have been calm, peaceful, 'safe' enough to the point that you felt it was time to share your true inner feelings. Now you begin to panic.

Dan appeared to show you that HE absolutely chose a new life just as though he had gone out and got hit by a truck. Remember how many times you've heard that the earth side is like a shadow side of truth, and that true colors exist on the non-physical side? In many ways, from actual colors to truth, you do live in a type of shadow. And what you so vividly received was a copy, from Danny, of your 'lesson plan,' so you went directly to him (at the 'morgue') to get the original. You did not accidentally wake up. Danny had already told you what he was going to tell you. The idea of a literal message at the end of the card was the 'message' you would wake up with at the end of the dream. You can love Jack without making love with him, because making love with him locks you into old habits, energies and manipulations. These old habits are your addictions, and your addictions bar you from your spiritual freedom.

From that day forward I worked diligently on these addictions. The rubber band on my wrist got snapped so frequently that it broke and I had to replace it several times.

THE END

Christmas 2006 came and went while I made plans to leave. Jack and I were together in the house during the quiet Christmas weekend, barely speaking to each other except when household logistics required it. He'd recently purchased a DVD player that could copy VHS tapes and make them into DVDs, and he busied himself with copying all our family videos, everything dating back to when each of our kids were born. At random times we'd end up in the living room together watching the old footage from opposite sides of the room, in silence. Watching and transferring these movies was our "swan song" in a way. It was a final but silent acknowledgment that there had once been a family here and that we would now be going our separate ways with our separate DVDs.

I mention this because another amazing revelation came through at this time. I watched all the years of my life with Danny on video tape, watched him walking, talking and playing, watched him on vacations and at family gatherings, watched all the fleeting moments of his life, and I found great joy in it, never shedding a tear. But I completely broke down when I saw the five-minute movie of my first skydiving experience.

I sobbed uncontrollably watching it, and cried not for Danny, not for my marriage, but for that woman jumping out of an airplane … my lost self. I saw who I once was, exuberant and vital, laughing and taking risks, beautiful and smiling and comfortable in my body. Danny was already in a wheelchair at that point, but I wasn't sad and neither was he, because Danny and I had found our own special joy. Even though Jack was living with us at the time and the relationship had been toxic for years, Danny and I were *happy*. We had each other, we had friends and family all around us, and we had a life full of activities, laughter and love.

But throughout those years Jack was consistently sullen, withdrawn and moody. He was the most gregarious and helpful guy on earth when people were around, but as soon as we were alone he'd be sulking again, moping around and snapping at me if I said even the most innocuous thing, such as "Wasn't that a great lasagna Stuart brought to the party?" He'd ignore me completely, as if he didn't hear me, staring straight ahead. If I asked, "Did you hear what I just said about the lasagna?" he'd respond angrily, "Yeah, of course I heard you, I'm standing right next to you." I'd hover there in confused silence for a few seconds wondering what to do, and then I'd say something lame, like, "I'm sorry (what was I sorry for?), are you OK?" And he'd get even angrier and say, "You're so negative. Why do you always think something's wrong? Nothing's wrong except how annoying you are when you start nagging me like this."

This was typical of most of our conversations. No matter how hard I tried to share positive energy and experiences with him, his fear and defensiveness overpowered everything. Engaging with him in a cooperative, interactive way was nearly impossible, whether it was a simple activity like cooking a meal or a major undertaking like a vacation (I was working as a travel writer at the time and was regularly offered free trips to great destinations). He was usually too busy to hang out with us at home, and routinely turned down the vacations. I was once offered a trip to

Maui for the four of us (Jack, Nicole, Danny and me), but he didn't want to go because he'd "been to Maui before and didn't see any reason to go again." No matter what, he kept his distance, remained withdrawn, bitter and alone, and blamed my "anger and negativity" for his unhappiness. So Danny and I went to Maui without him.

The skydiving images were a Christmas gift from Danny and Arlen. A picture of my true self, my *alive* self. And now that Danny was gone and Jack would soon be gone, the only disabled child remaining in my life would be *me*. Three weeks later I was making plans to file for divorce and start a new life 3000 miles away. During those weeks Danny talked to me a lot about the "Higher Self," and I realize now that these were pep talks to urge me on my way. Here are some of the things he said, with Arlen occasionally piping in when specific information about my marriage was needed. The following excerpts are a composite of what both of them said during this period:

"The Higher Self has no judgment. There's an ego self which is necessary for functioning on the physical plane, but the Higher Self is tuned directly into the plan it made with God before you came to earth, because we are not separate from God, we are *partners* with God, creating our plans as a team. The ego is ALL judgment, but the Higher Self has NONE. The ego makes decisions based on *'what will people think if I do this? What will I gain? How will I feel about myself? Will it hurt? Will there be guilt?'* But the Higher Self asks only, *'How does this serve the highest purpose for myself and for all beings?'*

You can always tell when information is coming from the Higher Self and God rather than the ego by using this simple trick... if it has no judgment, it's from God. If it feels like love and it resonates, it's from God. This is why those chants you've been listening to are so effective, because they focus the mind into that glowing core, that energy source, and it quiets the ego *[I'd been listening to a collection of meditation chants by a singer named Deva Premal... highly recommended]*. That's why you cry when you listen to those chants, because your ego takes a back seat and you feel nothing but the burning core. You know that information and guidance is coming from the Higher Self and God because it's done in a state of *love*, never in anger, blame or judgment. It's not difficult to recognize when your heart is truly open."

51

And this from Arlen ...

> "If you decide to leave your husband, do it directly from your heart, without blame or demonizing. Do it with great, great love, where your only wish is for both of you to grow and follow the intentions of your respective souls. It is Jack's choice to grow at whatever rate is comfortable for him. His wish to keep you in the marriage without examining its need for healing is based in fear; an ego structure designed to avert change. In this type of structure there is a winner and a loser rather than two people learning and growing from the conflict.
>
> By contrast, here is what a Higher Self structure would look like: We would have no requirements other than to be in complete, vulnerable, exposed truth at all times. We can work at jobs, raise children, be married or not, but we always look at the other person with unconditional *respect*, allowing them to be on their own path, offering love and also challenge when needed, but ultimately releasing them to their own truth, which means we trust that their motivations and actions are in the best interest of their own souls, which in a spiritual partnership also ends up being in our own best interest, because ultimately, we planned the whole thing together.
>
> We trust that plan in its unfolding, even though we don't know exactly what it is. Because trust between two people is merely an expression of the trust we have in God. If we're not acting out that trust in human relationships, we're not really trusting it on the higher planes. We look at every interaction and we don't ask, 'who's to blame?' We ask, 'is this statement or feeling coming from the Higher Self or from the ego?' Ask yourself this question with every action or thought."

GUILT, ANGER AND PURIFYING FIRE

When I first heard these messages about the Higher Self, I was encouraged by their truth and beauty. I had become adept at tuning into Heaven via meditation, but at the same time I was full of pain and anger, and like any mother who loses a child, I was also full of guilt. I knew I'd have to find a way to handle these emotions, to understand their role and put them into proper perspective, so one day I asked Arlen and Danny, "What about anger?" And they said:

> "Anger can be a fire that purifies, a form of energy that can burn a fire through you and motivate you to change a situation if you let it open you and then give it away to be transmuted into light. To judge your own anger is no different than judging another person, because you're judging yourself for simply experiencing your own plan. Anger can be a warning system that something needs to change. A very armored and defended person will be angry when they feel that their armor has been threatened and they will lash out in order to protect it. A person who understands that there's no difference between himself and others and that he creates all the energy he experiences, will welcome anger and work with it consciously because he understands it's telling him that something in his soul needs attention.
>
> Know this... anger should not be judged any more than any behavior or any action should be judged. Anger is the energy of fire and it can be cleansing and healing. When you feel anger, ask the fire of the anger to cleanse you. The power of the anger will dissipate and burn out and leave you inhaling the best part of that energy rather than projecting it outward onto another person. You can actually use it to bring energy up through the chakras and then give it to God. After you do that process you can come back and deal with the other person, cleansed and not projecting. As the anger burns its way up and out of your consciousness, the space will be filled in with the light of peace and healing."

I still agonized about whether or not to leave Jack, even though my soul was gently leading me toward making this change. I had come to accept that talking to him was pointless, but I still scraped the bottom of the barrel daily for any solution I could find, even though I repeatedly came up empty handed. I felt guilty about leaving and also about the ways in which I'd neglected Danny by being so distracted and obsessed with the relationship over the years. I had intense regret about what I perceived as wasted energy, energy that I could have given to Danny rather than squandering it on trying to fix and control my marriage.

Looking back on this now, I realize that I could not have moved forward with my spiritual work or the creation of a new life without having to experience a battle to the death with my ego. And what better emotion to lead the charge into that battle than *guilt?* No book written by

53

a mother who's lost a child would be complete without a dive into those dark waters.

The process of facing and ultimately releasing my guilt began with an incident a few months before Danny died. I'd decided that after Danny's departure I would have my last name changed to "Daniel" as a way to keep his name close to me (his actual first name was Daniel). I'd heard of people doing this to honor a departed loved one, and I thought it would be a beautiful tribute. I'd used several different names during my life for work and my public persona, and only started using my married name when I moved to Alabama. Jack always said he didn't understand why women have to take their husband's names when they married, and he never seemed to have a problem with the fact that I hadn't taken his until after we'd been married for more than two years. But when I mentioned my name change idea to Jack, his response was to say, "Oh, so now you've found one more way to put Danny above *me*."

Naturally I was appalled by this remark, not only because it was pitifully jealous, but also because it was a *lie*. Yet at the same time I was grateful for the lie, because it made me realize that the exact opposite had actually been true through the years. I'd been so obsessed with trying to make the relationship work that no matter what the cost to my well being or Danny's, I made most of my decisions based on what would keep the relationship intact. And Danny suffered because of it.

Danny must have felt fearful and insecure every day of his life, never knowing when peace and quiet was going to erupt into screaming and chaos, or when I would pack him up and take him away overnight to a friend's house or a motel to escape the insanity going on with Jack at home. How many times did I feed him his dinner while sobbing, or carry him into the shower while Jack and I were screaming at each other? And what was I thinking when I decided to move us to Alabama, away from Danny's friends, family, school and support system, for the distinct and exclusive purpose of trying to patch up my marriage? He must have felt so unsafe and helpless, not being able to walk or talk or take care of himself in any way. He couldn't give voice to his pain and fear. He just had to sit there and put his life into my hands. I was his lifeline, but I was emotionally unstable and I failed to provide what he needed.

I hated myself as I thought about these things. I was a disgrace. I had no boundaries and no *honor*. How could I disrespect Danny like that? I'd constructed an ironclad mechanism for denying that I was hurting him, and one of the highlights of my war with guilt was the realization that I'd sold myself a bill of goods, convincing myself that Danny was impervious to emotional pain. I'd put him on a pedestal, telling myself that he was an elevated, enlightened being, beyond the petty concerns of physical existence. Yes, of course he was an advanced being, but what I failed to acknowledge was that by living in an earth body, he had all the perceptions, experiences and emotions of any normal earth boy. I'd been telling myself that he wasn't really affected by the emotional violence around him, and that he was such a pure being of light that he could simply rise above it. What a crock of crap! I was despicable. I was the worst mother in the world. I had dishonored my son's *humanity*.

There were no answers available to me in the physical world, nothing to be gained by talking to friends, no advice a counselor could give and nothing in books, support groups or websites. I knew the only help would come from the higher realms, so I consulted Danny and Arlen. I told Danny how I felt about wasting so much energy on obsessing about my relationship with Jack, and that I was feeling paralyzed with guilt. And he said:

"You can already see and sense by writing those words how futile and unnecessary it is to feel that way. It was all as it should have been, exactly as planned. Energy can never be wasted. It goes exactly where it needs to go to fulfill your soul's plan. For example, one might say that some of my energy was wasted because I didn't have a high tech communication device that would have allowed me to type or input images to express my needs, as you recently read about in the book about the autistic girl, Adri. But I chose, with my free will, a disease that made that form of assisted communication impossible. I understood everything you said, but I didn't need to respond most of the time, because the silence served as practice for us to learn how to communicate telepathically like we're doing now. I did not choose to have 'facilitated communication' in my life.

The guilt you feel about this is important for you right now because it's part of the teaching that will take you out of your 'co-dependence.' Yes, you obsessed about the relationship and tried to mold it and manage it and force it to be something it could not be, and this is a big lesson for you. If this realization didn't hurt it wouldn't motivate you to change. Jack and I were the ideal participants for this lesson, because we pulled your energy in opposite directions so you would be forced to learn boundaries, self-esteem, release and acceptance. We were both impossible to fix or control. You could not fix my illness, nor could you heal Jack's personality disorder. And through this experience you learned about

55

forgiveness and release. You picked the perfect partners for your lessons in this lifetime. This was planned long ago in Heaven by the three of us."

OK. So much for my guilt about Danny. Now what about my guilt about leaving Jack? Not long after that last conversation, I laid down to meditate in Dan's room and got this from Arlen:

"You are looking for ways to help Jack, but your intervention will only short circuit a very important process in his growth. There is a parallel process going on for you as well... the stopping of destructive interactions with Jack and an addiction to trying to 'fix' him. It's true that Jack wants you to stop his pain by pretending that your relationship is acceptable the way it is, but if you try, it will only plug up one hole while forcing another to open, and the psychic bleeding will continue. You are not capable of plugging Jack's holes; only Jack can do that. Jack has given you power over his condition and you've agreed to take responsibility for his needs in that way. For years you found this flattering because it made you feel secure that he would continue to need you. But you've moved beyond that now and no longer wish to hold his power for him.

Danny sends you these 'scenes from a marriage' to introduce you to a new path. Notice that you're beginning to observe these scenes with love and a bittersweet sadness rather than anger. You're releasing more and more anger all the time. The pain and guilt you feel now isn't about Danny or about Jack. It's about the loss of old habits and familiar ways of coping that have been with you for many lifetimes. These habits are like old friends, and you're leaving them behind. It's a form of grieving.

Continue trying to talk with Jack if you wish, but do not expect conversation to resolve anything. That work can only be done in the realm of spirit now. Instead, use these conversations as a chance to practice compassion and love. Simply send him healing light. Picture him full of holes and send light through each one of the holes. This is all you can do for him. Work with him in spirit, soul to soul, because nothing you do on the physical plane will have any effect. Words will only confuse him and make him defensive, and comforting him with affection will only give him a temporary fix for his own addictions, which is no longer a responsibility you choose to take."

It's true what the great teachers say about this. If one person in a relationship transforms his or her own energy, the other person will either transform as well, or one of them will leave the relationship.

Because the ego can't survive in the light of the Higher Self

5. A New Chapter

"Although I'm in the non-physical and don't have the kinds of emotions that are familiar to you, I feel great love and longing for you, but not in a way that can be understood in the context of earth experience. I send love to your spirit as I know it in Heaven, the way you are on the other side, which is the true 'you.' You are only barely aware of this aspect of yourself while living on earth, but when I look at you from Heaven, it's all I can see. That's part of the reason why I'm helping you remember and connect like this, so that you can find that part of your soul again and teach others how to find theirs. I know who you are in Heaven, and I want you to know too."

Danny, from the Other Side

I am, at this moment, sitting in a beautiful rustic cabin in central Oregon, perched on the edge of a rocky gorge overlooking the Deschutes River. From the floor-to-ceiling windows on two sides of the cabin I can see nothing but the steep canyon, the high desert vista and the clear, flowing river. There's not a road, a car or a house in sight, even though there are neighbors all around and town is five minutes away. At night I can see lights on the other side of the canyon, which remind me that there are people nearby, but during the day there's nothing but the sky, the river, the geese flying overhead, my new dog Henry and *me*.

There's a fierce windstorm outside, blowing crazily through the trees and the wind chimes. It's winter, and I have a fire blazing in the big stone fireplace, and candles lit all through the cabin. There's Indonesian music playing on the satellite radio station, and there are photographs of Danny everywhere. I have never been more alone, but never more at peace. This place, my new home, is a miracle. Some would describe it as a perfect place for a writer to hide out and work on a book, but Elishevaa says it's an ideal place for a "contemplative," which is probably a very accurate description of what I am becoming.

Work and social opportunities are falling into my lap daily, and the world of spirit is at my fingertips whenever I call out for it. Last night I went to a workshop with a medium named Mariah Crawford, and although there were 15 people in the room hoping to connect with their loved ones on the other side, she tapped right in to Danny (he used circus images to get her attention). He's always right by my side. We're a team. I no longer doubt any of it.

How I came to find this place is a story for another time. Suffice to say that I asked for it and it showed up. Things are moving so fast, *time* is moving so fast, and I'm humbled with gratitude for Danny and his compadres every second of every day. On the six-day drive here he taught me, among other things, about "Heaven time," and now I understand how time can move so fast that it feels like you've been in a dream.

At this writing it has only been 21 weeks since Danny left his body. In that time, while still struggling to fit square pegs into round holes with Jack, a divinely-placed road sign fell at my feet, and it said, "turn here." It was not a detour, nor an exit, but a gentle yet firm directional indicator, straight from my helpers in Spirit. I filed for divorce, hired some guys to load my belongings onto a truck, and followed that truck on a 3000-mile trek from Alabama to Oregon.

Along the way I had one stunning spiritual revelation after another and talked into my little digital voice recorder constantly. I snapped the rubber band a lot too. I struggled with massive doubt and guilt as I prepared for my departure. But daily meditation and prayer, walks on the beach with Henry, talks with Danny and readings with Rebecca and Scott helped me to process it. I read every book I could find on channeling and manifestation and did every meditation and exercise I could think of. I cleaned my chakras, counted my breaths and healed my heart. I visualized a new home and a new life, and I visualized the manifestation of this book.

Leaving my marriage was far more difficult than caring for Danny during his illness and letting his body go when he died. It seems odd, but the reason is clear... everything with Danny was surrounded by love. The energy was clean and ego-free in all directions. By contrast, the relationship with my husband was cluttered with fear, resentment and projection. I snapped that rubber band so many times my wrist bled.

There's so much to tell and the information is so profound that I can't do it justice by using my own words. So I will use the words given to me by Danny and Arlen during my drive across the country. In this chapter I'm going to simply share excerpts from the conversations I had with Danny, my precious swan, and Arlen, his academic advisor. Some of what you're about to read includes musings from my own mind, but even those came to me in the form of transmissions from my guides. For the sake of easy access to these teachings, and because there is so much information, I've categorized these revelations from the road into specific topics.

BREATHING LIFE INTO THINGS THAT ARE NOT GOD

I left Alabama on a Thursday afternoon, armed with a pile of audio books by various spiritual teachers to listen to during the long drive to Oregon. My favorite of these was Carolyn Myss' *Anatomy of the Spirit,* in which she talks about the chakras and how they relate to symbols and practices from Hebrew and Christian traditions (for more about chakras, see Chapter Eight). When she described the fifth chakra being similar to the practice of confession, a light bulb went off in my head. I'd had asthma and other undiagnosed breathing difficulties for years, and I knew it was about the relinquishing of my VOICE during my marriage. It was obviously a fifth chakra issue, and Carolyn described it beautifully as "breathing life force into something that is not God."

Her words stopped me in my tracks. When I asked Arlen to show me how this related to my breathing problems, he told me that it's all about *breathing life into form.* If thoughts create reality, then breath infuses that reality with life. So during the years that I literally choked on my own breath when trying to express myself to Jack, it was because I was breathing life into a negative structure -- into a creation that wasn't God -- by trying to *force* communication into a space where it was not welcomed. Arlen reminded me, "you'll always know when your creations (i.e. your thoughts) are of God when they contain no judgment." During the weeks of planning my departure, I was in intense judgment about Jack because I had to rely on my anger and my wounds to propel me forward. I needed fifth chakra *confession* to release it. I thought I had forgiven him, but even forgiveness can be a form of judgment if it's about making another person wrong.

CHOOSING PERFECT PARTNERS

It's 3:30 a.m and I'm leaving a motel somewhere in Louisiana to get through Houston before morning rush hour. I listened to more Carolyn Myss and had a huge revelation about my work in this life. I came into this life with two gigantic fears... abandonment and being alone. My angels -- in support of my soul's plan -- sent me Jack, who would abandon me constantly, wear away at my self-esteem and keep me in a perpetual state of stress and self-doubt. Which means that he would work with me on a soul level so I could face those two fears every minute of every day. And I'm grateful for this. I came into this incarnation saying, "Who can I create that will help me do this work as efficiently as possible?" And I got Jack.

How interesting that this information comes on the heels of yesterday's revelation about judgment. I asked spirit to help me release my judgment of him and today I got this beautiful opportunity to do exactly that. I feel like I've just earned a post-graduate degree in forgiveness. And here I am, walking into the face of my greatest fears, choosing -- with joy -- to be alone after years of living in fear of that very thing. I'm finding out that being alone is not bad at all, because how could anyone ever feel alone when they know they're immortal and surrounded by immortal loved ones?

Danny had this to say about that:

"You purified yourself by making a conscious choice not to leave your marriage until you had forgiven, released and worked through your anger, blame and judgment. You knew that if you carried it into the next phase of your life you would not fully heal. And you've chosen to keep your heart open while learning to refrain from putting your energy into places that will hurt you. That's a delicate balance to maintain, because in the past you've mistaken the negative placement of energy for open-ness. You've mistaken protection for closing. You've believed that to love somebody you had to be so vulnerable that you had no protection at all. But that is not love, because it denies *self-love*. One of the gifts Jack gave you as your growth partner was to teach you how to protect your heart. What you did, from a spiritual perspective, was to choose someone who would injure you in order to strengthen that protection muscle. You're learning how to protect yourself from energy that comes from doubt and distracts you from God. This is a vital skill for someone doing Heaven's work."

HOW PRAYER WORKS

Throughout the road trip I had a series of problems with my dog, Henry. He'd been hyperactive and rambunctious ever since I found him as an abandoned one year-old puppy 18 months earlier, and life on the road was freaking him out. He's a high-energy yellow lab/chow mix, and was accustomed to our daily runs on the beach, so spending seven hours a day curled up on the seat of a mini van and then spending his nights in a motel room was unbearable for him. He'd been acting territorial and aggressive whenever strangers appeared, and one night he nipped at a motel employee in Texas. Company policy dictated that she had to be taken to the emergency room (even though he didn't break her skin), and that little episode cost me $400 for her hospital bill. I began to worry that Henry might be so out of control that I wouldn't be able to manage him. Knowing that my life might be unstable for the foreseeable future as I settled into my new surroundings, I didn't know if I could provide him with the secure home life he needed, and I considered dropping him off at a shelter and hoping he'd find a good home.

The thought of giving him up broke my heart to smithereens, and I cried all the way through New Mexico while beaming prayers out to God and my angels. I'd learned a whole new way of looking at prayer recently, and I completely understand when Carolyn Myss says, "Your relationship with God is not 'parent and child' as religion would have you think. Your relationship with God is a *partnership,* as co-creators working as a team."

So what I said to my team of God, guides and angels was, "Please show me the way to highest good. Let's work on this thing together, let's create this. Help me heal Henry." I asked to be shown the path to the highest good for both of us, and within a few hours, Henry's behavior and his energy started to change. The answer to my prayer wasn't to get rid of Henry; it was to confront the *possibility* of losing him, and then work through it to arrive at a whole other realm of possibilities.

I hadn't seen much of Danny in the last few days, but I suddenly saw him in the background, surrounded by his compadres, who stood with their hands behind their backs like soldiers at ease, and they're saying, "We're with you as always, but we're taking a hands-off position right now. You won't recognize the information unless you arrive there on your own."

I suddenly felt Danny behind me with his hands around my head, as if he had his hands over my ears. He was laughing (as usual), playing a game with me about holding the energy of my head in my hands. Suddenly I'm crying uncontrollably, feeling his presence, and my heart is expanding like a million stars exploding, like a starburst in my heart, and I realize it's that same feeling of openness that I felt on the beach the first week after he died. It's not a starburst. It's a "heartburst."

And now he's telling me that what I'm feeling in my heart right now is love, not pain, and that this huge, deep ache isn't heartbreak at all, it's *healing*. I can feel him healing my heart just like that day on the beach. It's the exact same sensation. I ask him to help me heal Henry, and the next thing I know I'm talking to Henry's soul, and Henry is lying there on the floor of the van sighing deeply, and I know that Danny is helping me. I very clearly hear Danny say:

"I'm giving Henry peace by giving peace to *you*. When you feel it, it will transfer to him effortlessly. God, the guides and you are part of a chain of command. Energy originates with God, then is received by the guides (myself included) and channeled through you to Henry, and ultimately to everybody else you touch with your love. You will become more and more aware of the way light and energy flow through you, ignited and maintained by God, which burns in all of us like a pilot light. You can be a conduit for healing Henry and others by doing exactly what you're doing right now... learning about the power of thought, which creates *everything*.

That feeling you get in your heart sometimes when we talk is a sign I'm sending you so you'll recognize my presence. In the future you may find yourself doing readings for people and crying, because this will be a sign that you're opening up to Heaven. I'm teaching you to recognize this sign, which you have aptly named a "heartburst." It's as if my energy is bursting through a membrane, just like the breakthrough image you refer to when you do Tarot readings [the card he refers to is "The World"]. Things are going to start changing fast now. Up until now a lot of our work together was mostly about me giving you comfort and subtle direction. You were in too much pain to do more than that. But now *you're* the one who's burst through the membrane, you're ready to go to the next step."

HEAVEN TIME

Driving through the gorgeous scenery in northern Arizona brought back a flood of memories about the years I spent with Michael, who was one of the great loves of my life. As I made my way along Interstate 40 I recognized landmarks from trips he and I had taken together, and was filled with sweet memories. I was shocked when I realized that it had been close to ten years since Michael and I had parted ways.

I counted back and calculated again and again, yet for some reason I couldn't believe it had been that long. It seemed like four or five years had gone by, certainly not ten. But of course it was ten. Michael and I broke up just prior to Danny's 7th birthday. And that's when it hit me... those last ten years were the exact years that Danny was sick, and the exact years that we spent with Jack! The onset of Danny's illness began literally the same month that Jack and I met. And now the relationship was ending just a few months after Danny's death.

Those years went by so fast, that to use a worn-out cliché, it was like a dream. It seemed that in the time it takes to fall asleep and have a dream, ten years went by. It felt like seconds, not years. And I had the strongest sensation that I had just woken up from this dream. These had been the ten most important years of my life, and I began to see that these years were bracketed in some way, set aside, apart from everything else. And Danny said:

"What you're seeing is something I'm teaching you about the nature of time. That's what time is like on the other side. And you're feeling an awareness of that, seeing these years from the angelic point of view, from the realm of spirit. You're not looking at them from the perspective of a physical body attached to earth experiences. What you're experiencing is 'Heaven time.' It's your soul boking at these memories, not your ego. Your soul is saying, 'How did I live my plan? Did I accomplish what I intended?' And looking at it from that perspective, you're aware that you wrote the story of those years into your growth plan, and that's how long it took to live that plan, mere seconds... as long as it takes to write a sentence.

Yes, the time you spent with Jack and me was 'bracketed' as you say. It was set aside because it was your master class, your thesis work in this life, it was the period where you would do the deepest work and move toward what you're supposed to do in this life. Because it was so clear, you found the souls you planned to do this

65

work with, and everything went as planned. This ten-year period after Michael was precise. It was precision living. Some people might look at this from the ego view and say it was the *worst* ten years of your life. But you and I know it was the best, because you see the gratitude and the purpose. You listened to your Higher Self and your guides. You got the time message. This is the message of time."

THE ANGELS WELCOME ME...
AND A LESSON ABOUT FEAR

The next morning I was traveling on Highway 50 in northern Nevada. A sign said, "Welcome to the loneliest road in America."

The scenery was beautiful, and I was the only person on the road, but far from lonely. I was listening to an amazing choral song on a CD that my friend Charlene had given me for the road. It was the word "Alleluja" sung over and over again like a mantra, to the melody of Pachelbel's Canon in D Major. It was stunningly beautiful, and I was singing along in a perfect state of grace and harmony when I had one of those heartbursts again.

The next thing I knew I was crying my guts out because it felt like angels were singing to me and welcoming me to Heaven. It was like that time at the chanting group when I heard *Ave Maria* and saw Paula coming to get Danny. It was the most ecstatic feeling I'd ever had. This was a huge moment for me because an hour earlier I'd been afraid to drive on this road. There was snow, ice and complete isolation to deal with, and I was truly afraid. I'd even stopped at a crossroads before turning onto Highway 50 and sat there for a good five minutes wondering if I should follow it. The thought of being stranded in the snow in the middle of nowhere with no cars coming by terrified me. But I decided to follow it anyway because it was the most direct route to where I was going (how symbolic is that?).

Five minutes down the road I had an intense hot flash, my heart started palpitating and I started sweating profusely, having visions of my little van broken down in the snow with Henry and me starving to death on the loneliest road in America. But instead of panicking and turning the car around, I laughed out loud and said to myself, "Wow, look at all the fear I have! How interesting!" And that was that. I just looked at the fear and laughed at it, and an hour later I was welcomed to Heaven by that beautiful song. Everybody was with me. It was too spectacular for words. My heart was opening up like a flower. I vowed to incorporate that song into a meditation. Amen! Hallelujah! Everything was perfect in the universe!

At around 3:00 in the afternoon I arrived in Winnemucca, Nevada and decided to stop for the night even though it was still early. I'd been driving since 5:00 that morning and was too tired to continue for the six hours it would take to get to my destination in Redmond, Oregon, and there were no motels along that route. I was looking forward to a relaxing evening, maybe taking a stroll through town with Henry, having a nice dinner somewhere and then settling in with my laptop to catch up on some work.

But my hopes for relaxation were shattered when I discovered that my laptop, my connection to the world, my best friend and my *livelihood*, had died a bizarre, unexplainable death sometime during the last 18 hours (it was working fine the night before). I'm more computer literate than the average consumer and can deal with many technical problems, but a "bios password issue" was way over my head. In fact, in the exclusive case of Toshiba laptops, nobody can "clear a bios password" except authorized Toshiba dealers, who have some sort of secret code or magic wand to address this freaky little glitch. After dozens of frantic phone calls I learned that the closest dealer was in Portland, ten hours away.

I was beside myself. The next day I would be arriving in Redmond and moving in to my new place, up to my eyeballs in boxes, setting up house, and dealing with other technologies like phone, cable and DSL service. There was no way I could go to Portland, nor could I imagine living without my laptop long enough to ship it there and wait for its return. The good news was that all my data was backed up on an external hard drive, which was securely packed away in my travel bag. I also had a "spare" computer that could help me limp through while the laptop was in the shop. So when I finally stopped cussing and crying, I prayed to my team.... "Why did this have to happen? Why now? Why on the last day of my trip? And why a bios password issue that nobody knows how to fix? What is the hidden message here, the hidden gift? What am I supposed to learn from this?"

What I couldn't anticipate at the time was that once I arrived at my new home in Redmond *all* my technology would fail. The DSL installation came with a program that was incompatible with everything else on my computer, there was a problem with the hard wiring in the house that caused my call waiting to disconnect the original caller every time I clicked through, my new email server turned out to be blocked by most of the major servers in America, and the Direct TV package I'd signed up for was a monstrous rip off. The whole thing was a comedy of errors and it was several weeks before

I could straighten it all out. I ended up sending the laptop to Portland where they fixed it easily, and thanks to my spare computer I was able to function almost normally.

Rebecca told me that this is a common occupational hazard for people who channel. Something about our attunement to higher frequencies has a tendency to interfere with electronics at times, causing them sputter out. These technology problems were so frustrating, such a hindrance to my life, that I found myself asking Danny and Arlen one day, "Why do we have to learn lessons? Why does it have to be difficult? Why can't we just hang out and do nothing? Where does that urge to learn come from?" They loved this question! And they gave me this very long answer...

WHAT WE'RE HERE TO DO
(and why we can't stop doing it)

"Because we are creators, because we are self-perpetuating balls of energy, we cannot NOT create. It is our essence, it's what we're brilliantly designed to do. It's almost mathematical, the way that energy reproduces itself. It has its own self-perpetuating life force. We are little burning flames fueled by a force called God, which energizes everything. We multiply upon ourselves, our energy is self-multiplying. This is why we are both the creator and the created.

The energy that we ARE resonates on an extremely high frequency, very much like the frequency of light. In fact, that's exactly what we are... *light.* That light is so charged that it can become energized enough to create matter. That energy is where thoughts come from, and this is why our thoughts have the power to create our reality and experience. We think a thought like 'it would be interesting to have a body and live in the physical realm,' and instantly that thought becomes manifest and we find ourselves in bodies. Because the more intention that goes into something, the denser the particles become, and the next thing you know you've created a physical form. At one point in time (though there really isn't any time), we all had that thought at the same moment, and boom, there we were, in bodies, living on a planet together. There's a constant, perpetual flow of energy that does nothing but just MAKE STUFF.

Because we can do that, because we had that thought and we came here, and because as soon as we came here we noticed that we were separate from Heaven, we then had to figure out how to *manage* what we'd just created. So we make experiences happen.

And the learning comes from this perpetual motion generated by that creative energy. We just keep generating more experiences and gobbling up more and more information from those experiences, and our souls love this (though the ego doesn't like it one bit). We just keep existing and creating.

The experiences, the creations, are going to happen anyway, whether we like it or not. It's what we're made to do, we can't stop it. So we may as well study it, work with it and play with it. Once we become conscious we see it almost as a game, and we can play with it rather than become too attached to it.

The next question is, do we really need bodies? Can our process of creating bodies just stop when we will it to?

Some believe that we need to have bodies until we arrive at a certain level of awareness and we're off the wheel of karma and we can't quit until that's done. But that's not true. We can do anything we want. Because we create with our thoughts and we choose a body, we can change that whenever we want to. We can decide not to have a body and serve as a guide from Heaven, or we can become another type of being or another life form. Everyone on earth at any given moment is part of a collective thought creation that says, "let's all live on this planet and have bodies." Remember this all happens in a blink of an eye, a day in the life of a creator. We can change the plan anytime we want to, but we can't stop existing because we are immortal beings. Can the ions in the air stop existing? Can light stop? That's what we are. We're light and particles and ions and thought forms. And we're *self-charging*, solar powered by God, the pilot light."

A PRECIPICE

Although I completely, without question, accept and believe that I'm truly receiving these transmissions from Danny, Arlen and others, I'm still in awe of it, and must admit there are times when I fear it will suddenly just shut off (there's that pesky fear of abandonment again). After I'd been in Oregon for about a month I worried that I hadn't been hearing them as clearly as I had back in Alabama and while I was on the road, and I was getting impatient. Then Rebecca gave me a reading with Elishevaa that validated everything I'd experienced and gave me greater faith in my ability to continue with this work.

They said:

There is great faith involved in this process. We understand very much your desire to clearly understand, but if the attempt to intellectualize or 'try' becomes too strong, it will indeed interfere with the ability to receive. Your part in the process is strong, devoted, daily prayer & meditation, supported by written journaling and communication with Danny and Friends. Yes, you do feel Danny and your other guides close enough to chat with, and you always will. However, that is very casual, and it is as far from what you will be able to do in the future as looking at a swimming pool from an airplane is to actually swimming in the pool.

Danny is grateful that his passing allowed you to disconnect from your old self. He knew it was time for his body to leave in order to allow you to do this very thing. You have, in your wonderful way, created symbolism for this cutting of the umbilical cord, changing your name, changing your living situation, and releasing your perpetual drama with Jack. Not only do you grieve for Jack and Danny, but truly the pain within is a release of many ancient energies.

There is a mourning period when ones release their old selves. It is the true meaning of 'born again,' and it can be a little disconcerting. Like a newborn, you put yourself into the loving arms of a universe you cannot see, and that is the meaning of faith. The mystical 'fruit of knowledge' that separated man from God/Goddess was ego. The realization of their own intelligence gradually caused ancient people to move further and further away from faith, because it did not seem logical. And it isn't. Until you give yourself completely to it, and then it is the divine secret–the ultimate knowledge that surpasses all.

Danny knew this and it was his hidden joy. Be gentle with yourself as you go through a far deeper change than the grieving of son and husband. A real spring cleaning if you will, from many lifetimes of resentment, and all justifiable, but no longer necessary. You are in a place that others can never quite understand, although you have great support. It is truly as though you are standing on a precipice, on firm ground yes, but inches from an enormous gorge of uncertainty. The winds are wildly blowing and you know you can fly, but you are also still afraid of the huge drop to the bottom even though you know you have nothing to fear. No one is standing on the edge with you, for that would be impossible. In the past, you have changed your mind and gone back to seeming safety, but it was not safe at all. It was a jail. Now, you will fly or die, because your son was willing to do so, and his strength is your motivation. And we know, you know, that you will fly.

God is with you dear one.

PART TWO

Heaven

6. Spirit Skiing

"All the truths, the secrets if you will, are always available to those living on earth, and these truths never change. Different beings on earth tap into them and express them at different times in different ways, but there can't be anything new because they're universal truths. Carl Jung referred to it as the Collective Unconscious, the Scientologists call it The Bank, or some call it the Akashic record ... it doesn't matter. It's universal energy and it's the raw material we're all made of.

When people write channeled books such as this one, they're simply *remembering* what they already know, with the help of guides and angels. By channeling like this you are remembering your ability to tap into the natural connection with God that we all have. When you hear these words and see these pictures, believe them completely, unconditionally and without hesitation. This will train your mind to accept other empowering spiritual ideas, such as a belief in safety, abundance and other truths that give you more command over your experience on earth. Each practice is a way of strengthening every other piece of life's puzzle. This is practice for learning to create your physical and emotional reality. The more you believe in your abilities in this area, the more you'll be able to accept the entitlement to peace that the universe offers."

Danny

Much of the material here so far has been focused on personal and human drama, and when Danny gave me the idea for this chapter, I suspect he felt the need for some comic relief. This chapter is filled with the playful antics of my beloved Swan in Heaven, as I recall some of the more lighthearted moments he's shared with me. It's a perfect way to begin Part Two of this book... with a smile and nod to the idea that beings in the non-physical have a sense of humor.

There were many times and many visions in which I saw Danny doing silly, playful things, like swinging on a child's swing set or gliding through the air on skis (he learned to downhill ski when he was five years old and excelled at it). Sometimes I see him bouncing around through a starry sky, leaping from star to star like Tigger from Winnie the Pooh. He's always laughing when he shows me these visions, and he often does this to make a point about how trusting in God and connecting with guides can be easy, light and *instant*.

Danny's heavenly frolics and cosmic capers are always mingled with profound wisdom, and sometimes he gives me deep, esoteric messages wrapped in incongruously festive imagery. These zany pictures often make no sense at all, only to reveal their true meanings weeks or months later when I "accidentally" stumble upon a person or event that brings the whole thing into perspective. This chapter is primarily in journal form -- with the entries in no particular order -- recounting unrelated events in which I saw Danny playing in Heaven, or "Spirit Skiing" as he likes to call it.

DANNY INTRODUCES ME TO SPIRIT SKIING

I was feeling lazy and non-productive because I hadn't come up with any new ideas for the book in the last few weeks. Suddenly Danny shows up ... *on skis!* He's skiing so fast that I can barely keep him in sight. He's like a beam of light zipping from here to there at warp speed, and his skis are making that swooshing sound even though there's no snow. I'm trying to catch up with him, to talk to him, but he's being really silly and laughing his head off.

I say, "I need help with the book. I don't know what to write next," and he laughs and says, "Don't worry, you will," and swooshes away in the imaginary snow. There are pine-covered mountains in this scene, but he's skiing *in the air*, not on the ground, and he's giggling with joy and abandon.

I ask him, "What is this? Hyperspeed skiing?"

And he says: "It's out-of-body skiing. I call it *Spirit Skiing*. There are no physical forces to control things like speed, distance and gravity, so I can move any way I want to. Wherever I desire to go, whatever speed or direction, I just think it and I'm there. It's like flying but much faster, and even though I don't really need the skis and the snow and the scenery, I like using them as props. I guess this is a form of recreation in Heaven. Do you remember the "Holodeck" from *Star Trek the Next Generation?* It's like that. We can create whatever we want."

And then I realized that this was his answer to my question about what to write next. I asked the question, and poof, there he is on skis giving me the answer. He wants me to write a chapter called "Spirit Skiing." I'm elated to realize how clearly and quickly my question was answered, and I'm so in love with this process, and with Danny. I thank him and tell him how much I love him. He tells me he loves me too, and he reminds me that we don't always have to talk about heavy things.

"Sometimes all I want you to do is to come play with me," he says. "You're right about the skiing chapter. It will make you happy and help you open the conduit more."

OK my love. I'll start writing *Spirit Skiing* today. Happy trails!

THE SWING SET

Eight days after his death I saw Danny playing on a child's swing set. He looked to be about 10 years old, about the age when he began to lose his ability to play like a normal child. He told me he was reviewing his life, year-by-year, as part of his entry to Heaven. I asked him which year he liked best, and he said:

"None are better or worse. I'm looking at the years of my recent life to check my progress, to see how I followed my soul's plan and to note any spots where I changed the plan or decided to avoid something or add something new. We can change our plans and make new ones any time we want to, and I'm studying mine to see if I copped out anywhere, to sort through what I need to work on next and to see where I've grown and what karma I've balanced. When you see me at different ages like this, I'm reviewing aspects of my life at that particular age."

FASHION MAGAZINES AND THE INTERDIMENSIONAL POSTAL SERVICE

In this meditation I saw Danny in what Sylvia Browne refers to as the "Hall of Records." I don't want to influence this image with what I've read in books, so I asked Danny to explain it to me and we engaged in a dialog that addressed angels, past lives and how humans came to earth. Danny explained:

"It's like a big library as Sylvia describes, but it looks different to everybody who sees it. I'm having a great time looking through books, looking up past lives to see what I might have missed or avoided, and choosing what I want to do next, the quantity and quality of the work I plan to do, like custom-building a computer and adding the components and features you need for the work you plan to do. It's like looking through a fashion magazine and choosing the clothes you want to wear next season.

I'm thinking about becoming some sort of doctor or healer. I've done this in past lifetimes, but I'm not sure yet about the form I want this healing work to take. I can choose to stay here and be a guide, to do healing work from Heaven, or I can come to earth and be a healer on the physical plane. When I was with you on earth in this last life, it was part of my training as a healer.[1] I don't have to go back to earth, but many of us choose that because we need to do something specific and we have contracts to honor.

In answer to one of your big questions, yes, there are angels, but they do different things than you imagine. They're magical, like fairies, they play with the energy and help to create light. They keep the energy clean, functioning like transmitters that move energy around, sending and receiving light. They are resonators for light and their job is to keep the frequencies clear. They look like fireflies, not like the pictures of angels that you've seen. They have many functions, but they are primarily keepers of light. You've heard about how angels help people, and this is true, but they do it with light. If a person on earth asks angels for help, the angels help by assisting the person to raise his frequency so he can receive and generate higher levels of light to guide and protect him.

By the way, Paula is here with me. She came to get me, just as you saw in your vision. She and I planned my birth with you and we're wrapping up loose ends here. We are taking care of Erika too and working with her energy."

ME: This is the best thing I ever experienced in my life. Thank you so much Danny. Do you know all your past lives?

"Yes, I can access all of them. I can look them up on something like the internet but without the hardware. I can easily retrieve them telepathically by calling for them. So can you, if you understand that you're capable of communicating with other realms and operating in

---

[1] I assumed he was referring his disability as a forum for giving him medical knowledge. But I learned in subsequent conversations that he was in training for a very different type of healing that had to do with personal issues and emotions. This is discussed in Chapter 10.

other dimensions. You can not only access past lives but also certain aspects of your plan for your current life.

Some of the plan can't be accessed because it isn't formulated yet. Your free will is still creating that plan, and there are always alternative possibilities. When you're aligned with your plan, things flow easily and when you begin to drift from it, from whatever experience you designed for your soul's highest good, you'll feel discomfort, which prompts you to change. If you ask God and the angels and your guides for help, they'll send you light and clarity, and mostly love, which you can feel. It makes you feel safer and stronger, and you can hear your soul more clearly and make the changes you need. But this requires a lot of faith. That's the true meaning of faith. It doesn't mean having blind allegiance to things you can't see or feel. It means the ability to listen to the messages you receive from your soul."

This got me thinking about how the internet mirrors our relationship with the non-physical. Using email as an example, a document leaves your physical space and travels somewhere. You can't see it physically traveling because it's in another dimension, which we've named "cyberspace." Most of us don't understand how it travels through cyberspace, but somehow it arrives at its destination. We can't see it or explain it, but it's part of our daily routine and we don't question it. Using the internet is an exercise in trusting that other dimensions exist. Danny explains:

"People with technical knowledge can explain it in terms of digital transmission, just like advanced metaphysicians can explain how we can "densify" light and energy until it becomes matter. Whether or not you understand it (how many understand how a television or a telephone works?), the internet is a wonderful but primitive example of communicating on other frequencies. It mimics the unseen energies that are constantly at work among beings everywhere, all beings, including animals and minerals. It hints at what you're capable of creating.

Before the internet you had access to information in certain forms, like books, telephones, libraries, television, movies, teachers, schools, museums and personal interactions with other humans. You didn't know there were other levels of access to information available to you, and if someone had suggested such a thing a

79

hundred years ago it would have seemed impossible. But now that a much wider world of communication has opened up to people on earth, it seems natural, and you take it for granted. You use it with *faith*. There are many more dimensions like this, and you're only just beginning to find them. The internet is a demonstration model that shows how inter-dimensional communication works.

The 'digital dialog' you experience when you're using the internet replicates how communication occurs across the various planes of consciousness, because you're made of light and you send signals in the same way. But most people on earth, because of the density of their physical forms and the incorrect teachings of most religions, can't comprehend or accept this."

Danny likes to use internet analogies because they're so applicable to today's world. Sometimes these analogies are deeply mystical and sometimes they're comical. One night Danny told me that he and I communicate through the "Inter-dimensional Postal Service" or the "IPS." He says that we send messages to each other via the IPS the same way people send physical packages via the UPS (United Parcel Service). Every time I see a UPS truck I send a psychic thank you note to Danny for this delightful image.

MAKING WEATHER

In the Spring of 2007 I was introduced to a series of books written by a boy named Matthew via communication with his mother 14 years after his death. I ordered the first book and sat down to read it moments after it arrived in my mailbox. I almost fainted when I read the part where Matthew's mother asks him if he's engaged in any sort of work in Heaven and he tells her that he's in "medical school." He goes on to describe how he's working with energy and studying a form of healing. This is not all that unusual except for one thing... six months earlier, before I'd ever heard of Matthew and his books, Danny said *the exact same thing* to me!

It was October 20, 2006, and I was enjoying the beautiful autumn day as I walked with Henry through downtown Odin. At one corner of town is the campus of a small southern college, a cluster of whitewashed antebellum buildings anchored by a larger building with a wrap-around front porch. A row of old-fashioned rocking chairs welcomes visitors to the porch, and I'd often stop and sit there during my strolls downtown. On this day I'd brought along my little voice recorder, and sure enough, Danny had a lot to say.

ME: What are you doing right now Danny?

"I'm making weather. I'm learning about healing and working very hard. I'm in deep study, like going to a sort of medical school. I'm becoming a healer, but using energy, not physical tools. By 'making weather' I mean I'm studying how to command energy with my will. Changing molecules, ions, particles and structure, shifting energy patterns and playing with atmospheres and environments. In medical school on earth one works with bodies, but it has less to do with the bodies than the energy created by—and attracted to—the souls inside those bodies. It's an advanced healing practice that involves changing the composition of matter by looking at it, listening to it and sending colors, light and sound to it.

These are our tools here, frequency and vibration. These studies can be used to heal life on earth, though I haven't decided if I'm coming back to earth any time soon. This is merely an area of interest to me, having been so sick in my last body. It's not like you perceive work or study or even meditation or revelation on earth. It's not hard or tedious... it's more like magic. Information just seeps in and it's very pleasurable to receive it. Everything just drifts into place and it's effortless. We can receive any kind of information we ask for.

In Heaven we don't forget our earth bodies. We actually honor them with great reverence, because they were important tools for us. Our bodies are perfect packages for living out our souls' intentions. It's not like we get to Heaven and suddenly earth is forgotten; it's quite the opposite. Our earth experiences are the drawing boards on which we work out our divine blueprints, but the work doesn't stop when the body dies. There's lots of work involved in making the transition from one realm to the other, and there's even more work to do when we get involved in life review, planning our next incarnations and helping others to do the same. It's joyful work because we created it, and the difference between growth work here and growth work on earth is that it's on our own terms here (so is life on earth, but most people don't understand that).

Here we recognize our own creations, and it's the most joyous work of all because it serves our individual souls and the collective consciousness of the whole creative and created organism. Every little piece of information, every experience and every revelation is wildly interesting, because we hold no judgments about anything, so no experience looks more or less desirable than any other experience. It's not better or worse to have a healthy body than a disabled body. It's not better or worse to live a life of comfort and wealth or a life of illness and poverty. The only value we put on the bodies is how well they serve our souls' plans for growth."

THE ORCHARD, THE DINNER PARTIES AND MEETING ARLEN

This was the day I had my first vision of Danny in his vineyard, the day he introduced me to Arlen. It was a stunning location that looked like a vast, wide-ranging farm, with vineyards, gardens and orchards stretching endlessly across the landscape. The light was amazing, a golden orange/yellow, and the air was dry and warm. It felt like the vineyards of northern California, but then I got a strong sense that it was Italy.

Years earlier a psychic I'd met in Maui told me that I'd find Danny in Italy after he died. I'd forgotten all about this reference, but now here he was, showing me this place, which I felt instinctively was representative of Italy. Later, in subsequent readings with other mediums, I was told about past lives with Danny in which our hands were stained purple from making wine. One medium said we had done this in Italy and another said it was France. It didn't matter, because this place, this blessed and magical place, was not on earth, but was an image he gave me of a Heavenly environment where much healing work would be done.

Danny led me through the gardens and said, "I want you to experience a peaceful, thriving world. Your soul needs to see this kind of energy today."

He looked younger, about nine years old, and when I asked why he seemed younger than he did during our last visit, he said that at this moment he appeared as a child because he's being loved, educated and nurtured by the people there, who are his teachers. Most of the people were up in the trees picking fruit, and the concept of the Garden of Eden flashed into my mind, as did the phrase "Tree of Knowledge."

At that moment I "heard" Danny say that he was being a receptor now, he was in study mode, receiving teachings from the great masters around him, and that's why he appears like a fourth grader. He felt *impressionable* to me, open, like an impressionable young child. He showed me this garden filled with the joy of learning, and people were busy with little tasks everywhere. I thought of Santa's workshop, and I laughed at myself for coming up with all these biblical and Christmas references.

One of the men in the trees caught my attention because he was exceptionally good looking (even on a guided tour of Heaven I still have an eye for a handsome man). Danny introduced me to him and I was quite stunned because I'd actually seen this man before in dreams and visions, though I can't remember where or in what context. Danny told me that this man is a special teacher of his and of mine, and I heard the name "Arten," but I doubted this name because it's the name of Gary Renard's guide from the book "The Disappearance of the Universe." Yet I heard the name so clearly that I was compelled to contact Rebecca and ask Elishevaa about him. This is what they said:

Loved one, the name we are receiving for this one is 'Arlen,' which is a name meaning 'pledge.' There has been a great pledge here, with you, Danny, your guides, your angels and your work. There was a time in Greece where you and Danny, both male, studied under this one as a teacher of Stoicism, but in this school he taught also of others, the great teachers and works of the time. He has incarnated with you in other times, mostly as a teacher, and he does so now in this time with Danny, taking up where they left off in their discovery of people, behavior, and events.

Part of Danny's experiment in his lifetime as a disabled child was a practice of Stoicism in its purest form, creating and controlling the inner experience without the ability to express outwardly in many ways. It was a peak experience for him to react to life in purity without willfulness, despair, or depression from lack of control. This is not to be confused with the simplicity of being stoic, for the teachings of Stoicism went far beyond that. You have great respect and fond memories of this time with Danny and Arlen, and part of God's great gift to Danny in this time is reviewing much of his work, processing this past life, with Arlen.

I sensed that this orchard/vineyard would become a sacred meeting place for Danny and me, and that Arlen and the others would always be close by. There was a little stream, and Danny sat there with me, holding my hands, not saying anything, just wanting me to feel his presence. Suddenly he looked older, and I knew it was because he'd switched from learning mode to teaching mode. He told me that we are always both teacher and student, and he also said:

"I will show you everything that I see. You can easily be in this place with me. Everybody can, when they're ready and when their hearts can open to spirit without judgment or fear. It's what Jesus meant when he referred to walking with him and knowing him. Before that can happen humans have to release their belief that they are separate from God. You can come here to visit me as easily as I can visit you on earth, because there is no such thing as 'here' and 'there.' We're together on many levels at once, and are not separated by time or physical space.

We will meet here and in other locales as needed, as we work together. These locales will represent something you'll be working on, and they'll change all the time. Eventually you'll understand how you are creating them yourself, and this will help to teach you about how thought manifests form. The little Serpentine heart stone you bought today represents your growth. It's green and verdant just like these vineyards and orchards. Serpentine has to do with guardian angels, and psychic energy pulses in emerald green light from the heart chakra. I'm in your heart and you can always call me to you. I'm here to help you learn to live from the heart."

He then showed me a scene of a dinner party in a house that sits on the land with the vineyards and orchards. The house is beautiful, a little stone cottage like one might see in a fairy tale. It's dark inside, lit by candles, and there's a huge stone fireplace. The dinner guests are brilliant people, gathered with Danny to work and teach together, and I realize that this is Danny's house. Arlen is there too, and Danny tells me that Arlen has introduced him to these others. They are a team, working together to help Danny, me and many others. Dan says, "The light is beautiful here. I've created a house and land and friends because these things are important to you and I knew it would be a setting that you'd love."

At this point we began the following dialog, which jumped all over the place to multiple topics, but was filled with fascinating information, much of which didn't make sense until much later, when subsequent visions and experiences validated what was being said:

ME: What's going on at the dinner party? What do you talk about?

DAN: It's like a strategy meeting. We're sitting around with maps and charts and planning our next life together. These are people who've been with me a long time, like guardians and members of my soul family, and we're working together, planning when and how we will meet again. You and I have sat at this same table at times, doing the same thing.

ME: Sylvia Browne says we can't incarnate any sooner than 100 years after our last physical death, but that doesn't ring true to me. *Conversations With God* says we can do it whenever we want. Which is true?

DAN: It depends on your level of growth and your plan. The process of growth determines everything, and you can grow at whatever rate is comfortable for you. Sometimes we can choose intense lives filled with hard-hitting lessons, and at other times we can take it slow and not have too many life-changing challenges. You plan to come in at certain times, like next week or a thousand years from now. The time periods in which you choose to be born have to do with the cultural and historical influences needed for your work on earth. There are no rules about time, because in Heaven there is no time. And we don't have to necessarily go to earth. We can go to other planets. We can stay here. We can do anything or go anywhere, which is why we don't get bored in Heaven. Because there's no time, there's no impatience or concern about what to do next. Everything you could want or imagine is right here the moment you want or imagine it.

ME: What are you planning? Will we be together again?

DAN: Yes, absolutely. We've been together many times and we have much more work to do together. We are going to be healers together again, just as we were in my most recent life. In that life, me with my MLD and you as my mother, the work we did as a team, do you not think we had the role of healers? It didn't seem so to you at the time, but we healed not only each other, but also many of the people we loved and the people you taught in your spiritual groups. This book we're writing now is an act of healing. I plan to be with you and work with you, but I'm still not sure if I will work as a healer in the physical or not. You'll be interested to know that whenever I do come back to earth, I'm considering the option of a lifelong happy marriage with someone you know, someone who is here with me now (I was hearing the name "Shanna" or "Shaina").

85

ME: Do I know this person from my current physical life?

> DAN: You have not been in her physical presence during your
> current lifetime but you have been aware of her, psychically, from
> time to time. You have worked with her in spirit at other times. Her
> soul's name is Shyla[2].

MORE ABOUT LIFE IN HEAVEN

I had begun speaking with Arlen regularly. He told me that he will be a
guide for me, that I can be with him easily whenever I want to, and that he'll
be part of the book I'm writing with Danny. He took me on a grand tour of
Danny's home in Heaven, this place in "Italy," and gave me some basic
explanations of the work that goes on there.

The little cottage is small because most work is done "outdoors."
There are fields everywhere, and the sea is in the distance. It looks
almost like a scene in a Tarot card, but not a card I've every actually ever
seen. I learned much later that everything about this place is symbolic
and representational of either something Danny is learning or something he
wants to teach to me. The images I see of people working in the fields and
carrying baskets of harvest are symbolic of the spiritual harvesting they're
doing as helpers to beings on earth. Arlen told me that I would see and work
with Danny in many other settings, according to the specific type of work
we'd be doing.

Arlen explained to me that Danny's new "home" has gardens and
orchards but they don't need to eat, yet they can eat if they want to, simply
for the sensual enjoyment of food. They can manifest rain, snow or
sunny days, whatever they choose. Their work in this environment is to
serve as helpers and teachers to people on earth and to beings everywhere
who are connected to their network of information and energy
exchange. Between incarnations we all take turns in different roles, as
helpers in Heaven or helpers in physical form, with thousands of variations
in between. Arlen told me that my friend Rebecca is an example of someone
who works between the worlds, which is why her life here on earth is so

---

[2] I looked this name up and was delighted to find that it means "Goddess"
in Sanskrit.

challenging. She's a "Heaven helper," he said, in a physical body and not always sure where she belongs.

Beings in Heaven can keep very busy if they choose to, and Danny, Arlen and our soul family are a group of working healers who are available to anybody who asks them for healing and light. They can amuse themselves in any way they like, and Danny enjoys gathering people around the large dining table in the cottage and having "dinner" parties. He also likes female companionship and has many loving female energies around him (no big surprise there; he was surrounded by a female fan club all through his life on earth). There is a powerful personal communion that occurs between beings, but it's not sexual or carnal, doesn't have physical sensations, and of course isn't tied to reproduction in any way. It's more of a deep, psychic recognition for the purpose of mutual vision and soul work. There are no exclusive attachments or jealousies because these bonds aren't based in the ego nature like they are on earth, so there are no insecurities or possessiveness. Everybody knows that they're loved completely and unconditionally by everybody else and by God, so nobody feels abandoned or injured when a friend moves from one bond to another. The love is so universal that nobody questions its abundance… there's enough for everybody. There is only one true bond, and that is the Divine Love that connects us all. This is one of the biggest lessons that guides try to teach us here on earth. We are capable of experiencing that same universal love even while in these bodies. It's the essence of our true spiritual nature and the natural state in our Heavenly home. When Arlen taught me this, I arrived at a higher understanding of what the Course in Miracles means about there being no "special relationships." There are unique, exclusive *experiences* with various beings, but the relationships are all equal in love, learning and acceptance.

Danny has the stature of a great landowner and grandfather here, a loving patriarch with many friends, students and teachers around him. It is not *his* home exclusively, but a home he created for our soul family, and he's delighted that I have the ability to visit there. He's looking particularly strong and handsome today as I see him walking around smiling at people, puttering and tinkering with things. Arlen is there with him and they are all working together. I ask Arlen if the idea of Italy is just because of the image given to me by the psychic in Maui many years earlier, and he reassured me that the psychic was correct, that Danny and I have past life connections to Italy.

In that reading, the psychic said that Danny had been an opera singer in a past incarnation (I often wondered if this explains why he responded so well to songs when he was losing the ability to communicate with words). I remember clearly how one evening a few weeks after the Maui reading, I put on some opera music to see how Danny liked it. He could still talk back then, and after we listened for a while I asked him what he thought of the music. He replied emphatically, "I *love* it!" How many 11 year-old boys would say that?

KALI MA

After my first visit to the chanting group when I saw Paula coming to take Danny to Heaven, I began attending the group regularly. One evening John led us in a high energy chant to the Hindu goddess "Kali," who represents the energy of fire, creation, destruction and re-creation. I still wasn't too fond of chanting, but I liked the people in the group and the energy of the chanting, and on this night, the "Kali Ma" chant, accompanied by hand clapping, was passionate, loud and very high energy.

For some reason this made me laugh. Something about it was riotously funny to me, and I couldn't keep a straight face or align myself with the reverent deportment of the other people in the room. So I decided to just give in to my laughter, and when I did, I was instantly able to see the source of my amusement.

It was a vision of Danny, Arlen and everybody else I know in Heaven, including my dog Jackson, Paula, my grandmother, my dear friend Sydney and dozens of others, dancing around a big bonfire to the sound and rhythm of the Kali Ma chant. They were laughing too, and it was beautiful, but utterly comical at the same time. It was almost as if Danny and his friends were making fun of the chant, as if they were saying, "these silly humans chant to external gods, and all they really need is to know that the energies of these gods are *within*. But hey, this is what Terri's invoking right now, so let's share it with her." They weren't *making* fun, they were just *having* fun.

In a meditation later that week, I saw Danny, Arlen and some others sitting around the table in the cottage. Danny had his feet up on the table, pushing back in his chair like kids often do. He looked so beautiful! I realized they were having a conference about *me*, and I was an honored guest at their table. They told me they were indeed dancing that night during the Kali Ma chant. The chanting brought in a lot of fire energy, they said, and it inspired them to dance around a fire. They wanted to let me know that beings in Heaven can hear chanting like that because it's very effective at raising the frequency of the chanters. Kali Ma is a powerful ancient chant that has survived through the centuries and is used commonly in Hindu prayer. Arlen said:

"I know you've seen a lot of seekers, false teachers and others using these ancient spiritual words and chants, and they've become distasteful to you because they've been overused and/or misused, just as certain western words like God, prayer and spirit had once become distasteful to you. But look how that's changed, and how you now understand these words for their true meaning! You now speak them with joy and reverence, and this change happened automatically and easily, simply through the process of opening your heart up to Heaven. Over time you will come to embrace some of the ancient Sanskrit and Islamic words as you continue in this work and as you become more familiar with their vibrations."

And he was right. Over the next year many of these words became part of my everyday vocabulary.

BLUE, WHITE, GREEN AND THE PLAID SHIRT

In the midst of formulating a plan to leave my marriage and start my life over again, I had the following conversations with Danny. I hadn't yet decided to move to Oregon, though a dear friend in Portland had invited me a surprise party she was throwing for her husband's 50th birthday, and it seemed like a good opportunity to take a look around the area. I had no fixed ideas about where I would relocate. Oregon was a possibility, but so was California, Arizona and a house on 40 mountain acres on the Alabama/ Georgia border. Trying to make these decisions drove me crazy, and I was filled with doubt, until I learned to release the decision-making process entirely and do nothing but meditate and allow divine guidance to lead me. My conversations with Danny during this period address all of these questions and much more:

ME: What are you doing right now Danny?

DAN: I'm looking at a forest, seeing landscapes and thinking about how I want to come back to earth. When I talk to you it brings

89

me back there, and I don't really mind it. I like the forest and the air and the beauty of earth. Right now I'm showing you a pine forest.

He shows me a snow-covered pine forest on a clear, sparkling day. It's viewed from an interesting perspective, as if seen through the lens of a movie camera positioned on a helicopter, slowly pulling back, revealing a wider scene as the camera moves farther away. Danny is pulling me into the sky with this vision. He's laughing and I hear him say, "Blue, white, green." My heart jumped at these words, and my eyes filled with tears of joy and recognition, because "blue, white, green" was a favorite old joke of ours.

When Danny was about six years old I told him a story about a friend of mine who'd tumbled down a mountain in a skiing accident. My friend had described what she'd seen while falling through a swirling vista of trees, sky and snow as "blue white green blue white green blue white green, over and over again." Danny always found this story hysterically funny, and for years I could just go up to him and say, "blue white green" and he'd dissolve into giggles. Now, from Heaven, he was reminding me of our little joke. I also realized that the ever-widening camera angle was the view from a ski lift as it goes up a mountain. He was sharing his fond memories of skiing from when he was a little boy!

I wondered if these images were answers to my prayers about where my new home would be. I'd been considering the city of Bend, Oregon, and I asked Danny if this was the place he was showing me. He said, "No, but it's near there." I learned later that Bend itself is not located in a dense pine forest, but the areas around it look exactly like the pictures Danny showed me. I couldn't have imagined at the time that seven months later I'd not only be living in that area, but building my own home on a lot with a view of pine trees and snow-covered mountains.

I told Danny that the thought of moving across the country alone terrified me, and asked why this particular move seemed so much more frightening than the move to Alabama two years earlier. He said:

"You're afraid because you're finally taking an irreversible stand with Jack, and also with yourself. This is a huge risk for you, because it will change your life and your way of seeing things forever. But this is what it feels like to truly own your life. Yes, you will be alone in a sense, but not in the way you imagine. You'll have lots of friends there, and you'll always walk with me and your angels and guides, so you can never truly be alone. You'll eventually find a

90

new mate, but not until you've completed a large piece of growth work according to your soul's plan, and strengthened yourself so that you'll never need a chaotic relationship again. What will be different is that you'll lose an old identity.

When you moved to Alabama you had me, a disabled child, and I was your ticket into some very accepting, loving groups of people. You knew that anywhere you went you'd have a community and a place to belong... with parents of special needs kids. I was a sort of flag, an identity that set you apart and made you special. Being my mother gave you a unique and lofty purpose, which attracted support and admiration to you. Without me, you're afraid that you won't be able to attract that on your own, but what you don't realize is that you will become even more magnetic to the right people, because you will create a new purpose, and will stand strong for that purpose.

During the last nine years you identified with being the mother of a disabled child and the partner of a brilliant but disturbed man. But now you have the opportunity to identify with nothing but your own Self and its creations. There's nothing to hide behind. And from that place you will become more powerful than you can imagine. You will attract right livelihood, friends, community and eventually a life partner who will love and recognize you fully for who you are and what you contribute to him and to the world. You are going to be something brand new."

Obviously he was in teaching mode during this speech, and I noticed that he was looking more handsome than usual, a bit older, and wearing an orange and brown plaid flannel shirt. I asked him why he was wearing that shirt, and he said, "It symbolizes Oregon because that's what those lumberjack guys wear out there. I'm giving you the sign you asked for to let you know that it's OK to take this exploratory trip with your friend in Portland."

I was relieved to have this clear sign, but had no idea how to take the first step.

ME: How do I do it Danny? How do I make this happen?

DAN: By not forcing it. Allow it to unfold. Stay close to your guides as usual. Love Jack all you want, that's part of the process, because you can't release him without loving him. Work on releasing blame, resentment and doubt. Meditate on forgiveness daily. The

91

only way to do this is to open your heart, but it will not open with too much anger present. So release everything, pray, meditate, and look at Jack with love and compassion. Follow everything your heart says, even if logic says no. In the end, with each experience, the heart will prevail and show the way. The more open your heart becomes, the more able you'll be to hear divine guidance and to communicate with me.

THE TINKERBELL EXERCISE

This was one of the most playful experiences I ever had with Danny. I was in a terrible state of anxiety, worrying about the details of my move across the country and agonizing about Jack. It was 3 a.m and I was lying awake in absolute misery. I tried to meditate but nothing would gel, I couldn't calm down, had no luck reaching Danny and just wanted to scream. I was trying way too hard to connect, and pleaded with Danny out loud, "how can I reach you when I'm in the middle of a logjam like this?"

Within seconds of asking this, my thoughts shifted away from expectations of having deep conversation with Danny and moved into the realm of ordinary maternal love. I don't know exactly how it happened, but I just started thinking about Danny's sweet face, remembering how it felt to hug him and kiss his little cheeks, and I just lay there doing nothing special, just feeling the love I have for him without looking for deep conversation or anything complicated.

And I realized that *this* was his answer. He was showing me that all I have to do when I'm in an agitated state is simply tap into the love I have for him and he'll show up immediately. And he showed up in a big way, saying:

"Feel your love for me and mine for you. Don't ask questions or think about topics or issues. Just think of me; look into my eyes the way you'd look into the eyes of a rescuer, as we've talked about before. I'll steady you and focus you if you open to love and think of nothing else. Feel the vibration of your love and the vibration will carry you to me. We don't always have to talk about deep things. Sometimes you can just come out and be in my energy, just to hang out, with no particular plan or purpose. Just to be inside my energy."

So of course I did what he told me, I released myself to that, and imagined hugging and kissing him, imagined his eyes and felt his presence. And then I suddenly saw him dancing and flying through the night sky, giggling, playing and showing me a picture of pure, unbridled joy. He was still wearing the orange plaid shirt, laughing and being really silly, and he was reaching out to offer that energy to me. A sudden stray thought about Jack crept into my mind at that moment and Dan noticed it immediately, and said:

"There is no need to bring him into this space with us. This is an exercise for you to experience what it feels like to be free of all painful memories and all thoughts of Jack. I have my own relationship with him, and he and I will deal with it ourselves. You no longer have to be in the middle. The three-way link is broken for now, and he and I will work our relationship out on our own. You don't have to worry about it anymore."

We continued to fly together through the stars, and he was bouncing around from star to star, spiking beams of light on everything he touched. It reminded me of Tinkerbell in the opening sequence of a Disney television show from the 1960s, where she tapped things with her wand and they opened up in bursts of light. I felt unbelievably free of my earthly concerns. Danny was taking me on a journey to show me how it would feel to finally be free of the stress, chaos and confusion that had been the mainstay of my life for so long. What a beautiful gift! I'd been so agitated, so in need of soothing and sleep, and as soon as this interaction with Danny occurred, I was instantly calm and drifting off to sleep.

As I fell asleep I heard him say:

"I love you mom, and I'm having so much fun working with you like this. Don't worry about losing this connection. You are *always* invited to the dinner party."

7. The Gratitude Channel

"God only gives, never takes away. When you feel that something has been taken from you, a beloved fiend or pet, a job, or even if your house is blown away in a hurricane, it is actually a gift from God to propel you toward a much-needed change that your soul has been craving, though your ego self might have no awareness of that need. The next step in your life, the thing that your soul not only desires but planned as its next step, could not happen unless the thing you lost was 'taken from you.' The truth is that God only gives. The illusion of having something taken away is nothing more than an opportunity to practice forgiveness and release and let your soul follow its growth course."

Danny

Today Danny introduced me to "The Gratitude Channel." He told me that gratitude is the natural state in Heaven, and this is why telepathic messages are given so much more freely to us by guides and angels when we're in a state of gratitude, because gratitude strengthens the connection between dimensions. It bridges the gap between creation and experience. It opens a gate that is blocked by fear in physical life. Any energies or beliefs that are not based in gratitude are based in fear.

Most people think of gratitude as something we express when a friend does a favor for us, or at Thanksgiving dinner when we voice our thanks for the safety and comfort of our lives. While this is a certainly a form of gratitude, there's also a more metaphysical form that holds us accountable for all our creations and experiences. And whether these experiences are perceived as "good" or "bad," being in a state of gratitude for them gives us ultimate ownership of them, and thus a greater sense that we have some control over what happens to us. Gratitude is *empowering*.

I said to Danny, "This is a difficult concept for people to understand. How can I explain that we have to be grateful for our so-called negative experiences? Maybe it would be easier to explain if you could define the *opposite* of gratitude. Perhaps if people could understand what it *isn't*, it would be easier to understand what it *is*."

And he replied instantly, without missing a beat, "Your *will* is the opposite."

It's important to clarify that this should not be confused with *free will*. The "will" Danny's referring to is more like obstinacy, a blinding human need to control circumstances, outcomes and other people. Most of the time we desperately attempt to fend off uncertainty at any cost, and are unable to simply BE with discomfort long enough to truly deal with it. It's difficult, if not impossible, for most of us to recognize that change and upheaval are gifts rather than tragedies. We tend to live in a fiercely protected stance, feeling victimized when things aren't easy or safe or happy, and there is great pain as we struggle to understand why these "bad" things are happening to us.

Gratitude, by contrast, allows us to receive and accept energy and experience without judging it as *good* or *bad*. This doesn't mean that we're supposed to passively let the world bulldoze us into submission. It means that we can look at each event and each experience as one of our creations, a precious gift in a form that gives us vital information about what to do next. It's not that we're supposed to say "thank you Spirit for the heart attack I just had." It's more like saying, "thank you Spirit for the way in which this heart attack will move me forward in my soul's intention."

Danny explains:

"In a state of Gratitude you accept everything with love because you recognize that it is your own creation. How can you not love your creations? To not love your creations is to believe that they come from somewhere outside yourself, as if some unseen force is moving you around like a slot car and you have no say about it. To not love your creations would imply that they are somehow imperfect and need to change or disappear. So you try to change or fix or erase them, believing they need changing, fixing or erasing. And in doing so, you end up living in a state of resistance to the very thing your soul created from love. You resist everything that your Higher Self is trying to teach you, and this is the "will" I speak of. This resistance is quite painful, and is the opposite of gratitude. You should not be so quick to push difficulty away or to cover up or medicate the pain in life. These things should be listened to, honored and embraced. They are direct messages from God, the angels and your own soul working as a team of co-creators.

As an example, let's say something terrible happens, perhaps your dog gets hit by a truck, and you're devastated and grief stricken. It seems inconceivable that there could be gratitude in that. But if you are a person to whom connection with Spirit is more important than anything else, the gratitude, while not immediately apparent, can be realized via prayer and meditation that asks to see the truth and the purpose of the situation. You will realize that God didn't take your dog away. God gave you an opportunity for change, because if you can process this painful loss without scrambling to cover it or rush through it, you will find yourself on a much higher plane. Life does not stagnate. Growth always seeks to happen. The path is always changing, and pain is one of the most powerful triggers for change. In this sense you learn to be grateful for every experience that moves you forward.

God only gives. God never takes away. Every experience is a gift, a stepping stone on the path of the soul's growth. Perhaps in the dog scenario you get a chance to feel your feelings for once in your life if you've been a person who's always shut them off. Perhaps you take the dog to the vet and the vet turns out to be the person you marry. Perhaps you sink into a pit of anger and rage, and in that pit you face personal demons that could not get your attention any other way than to access you when you're blown open by shock and pain."

Danny used the example of a dog getting hit by a truck because I'd been praying about that very thing just a few hours earlier. I usually take Henry to walk with me up a little mountain near my house called Cline Butte. There's a rock quarry up there and large trucks come barreling down the mountain road all day long. We walk on an obscure dirt trail up the butte, but Henry has been known to wander off and end up dangerously close to the road where the trucks are. On this particular day I was particularly worried about that road and those trucks, and my fear was so strong that I had to stop and meditate to get an answer... should I skip our walk up Cline Butte today? But if I *do* go there and a truck *does* hit Henry, then was it meant to be?

I pondered this question for a long time, listening intently to the nervous feeling in my stomach. Thanks to what Danny's taught me, I've developed a unique understanding of prayer, and it's a world apart from what most of us learned in Sunday School. Most people have the idea that we're supposed to ask God for intervention, for favors and gifts, particularly when we want to stop something bad from happening (there's that pesky will again). But if these so-called "bad" experiences are created by our higher selves to teach us important lessons, then instead of trying to stop them, why not ask instead to *understand* them? Why not simply ask to hear, see and sense the highest truth in the situation?

So on this day, as I tried to figure out whether or not to walk up Cline Butte, I said in prayer, "show me the highest truth for the greatest good in this situation." It was an exercise in surrender. I was open to all possibilities and put my complete trust in divine guidance and my inner voice.

As soon as I asked the question I got a strong feeling that it was OK for Henry and I to walk, and it was during this walk that Danny began talking about The Gratitude Channel. The whole purpose for my fear and my prayer was to open my mind to hearing Danny speak on this subject.

THE MECHANICS OF GRATITUDE

Interaction with divine energy happens on many different frequencies, on different channels, like tuning in to different radio stations. There are thousands of these channels located at different levels of consciousness, and each channel has a specific purpose and characteristic.

Extreme emotional pain is one of these channels because it opens your heart, and in this open state you can surrender completely to God if you choose to. Grief does the same thing, and on this channel there's a lot of work to do that has the potential for tremendous growth and healing. Breathing is a channel, as are levels of deep meditation, prayer and chanting. Each of the chakras is a separate channel, and forgiveness is most certainly a channel. Dreams are extremely clear channels. Other channels are art, music, dancing, crying, playing, nurturing, sexual love, brotherly love, spiritual love... the list is limitless, and everything that comes to us via these channels is manifested in some form in our physical lives.

For example, if you're a visual artist, you have an image in your mind and a need to express it so that others can see it too. You paint the image on a canvas and when it's finished, your creation comes to life. If you take this one step further and somebody buys the painting, you're not only able to support yourself financially from it, but you've now connected to another person who resonated with your vision enough to buy it.

The same is true with music, writing, weaving, dancing, teaching, raising children, planting flowers or cleaning your house. We are manifesting our creations constantly on all these channels of creation. Birth, death, grief, falling in love, falling out of love, anger, laughter, sex, the connection you feel when you're in harmony with animals or nature... all of these transitions, layers, levels and dimensions are the creation channels on which we operate.

Now imagine yourself saying, "Thank you God, thank you guides, thank you for sending transmissions that I, in my power as a creator, have manifested as this painting or this new baby or this batch of fresh baked cookies." Why wouldn't it also be true for other manifestations, such as an accident on the freeway or an illness? If you can learn to see all your creations equally, saying the same prayer of gratitude for all of them, you'll be amazed at how much faster and more efficiently your creations will manifest and how much more command you'll have over them. The more gratitude that flows through this channel, the more empowerment you receive in return. When you operate on this channel you receive stronger messages from your soul because you're not judging or resisting those messages. And the more easily you receive them, the more powerful your responses will be in terms of manifesting what you envision for yourself.

This energy travels in both directions. The messages come to you from a divine source (your Higher Self in partnership with God, angels and guides) and your creations automatically burst forth. Those messages trigger the changes in your life, including the painful and traumatic ones. Hopefully you can receive them with gratitude instead of resistance (you really have no choice, because they're going to manifest anyway, whether you welcome them or not). The trick is to receive all of it—joy and sorrow—equally.

If you can begin to see things this way, you'll soon realize that your experiences don't fall randomly out of the sky. You will know that you actually *create* them, and you will have gratitude for the miracle of seeing your creations manifested in physical form. Your soul is saying, "I had this idea a thousand years ago (or ten seconds ago), and now here it is in front of me. How awesome!" If we truly have no judgments, if we are truly in the Heaven mind, that's the only reaction we could possibly have. If you ask, "How could this terrible thing happen to me?" it means there's no recognition of it as your creation. There's only resistance and pain.

But when you recognize your soul's creations, it's as if you build a house and choose the paint color, and when it's all done you look at it and say, "Wow, look at what I created." If you don't like the color, you don't blame someone else or feel victimized. You deal with it, you move on and you grow in the process.

In gratitude, a powerful state of grace, you can have a car wreck and you can receive it, you can forgive it, you can forgive the experience, which, as the Course in Miracles says, will happen when you realize that the experience and the people involved in it are not separate from you. You have the recognition that "Oh, here we all are, the guy who sideswiped me and the police and the ambulance and the pedestrian who is now dead. We agreed to meet here at this moment and do this. This was a creation of mine and of theirs, of all the people who interact with us, a creation designed to move us all forward to a next step."

Now *that's* heavy. Not many people can feel that way at the scene of a tragic accident. It's an uncomfortable and unfamiliar way of thinking. And it gets even more interesting when you discover that the Gratitude Channel lives right next door to the Forgiveness Channel.

Danny summarizes it much better and more succinctly that I can:

"When you begin to understand that we are potent light sources that can create matter and manifest anything, then no experience can be judged as 'good' or 'bad.' You can only have gratitude for seeing your creations coming to life. From this perspective you are connecting with your Higher Self and with all the energy in the universe by way of a very specific channel, which we are calling 'The Gratitude Channel.' Not only can you receive guidance effortlessly from spirit on this channel, but you'll be delighted to discover that it's actually bi-directional, and you can send information back and forth. When you send gratitude back, you're trusting that all is as it should be. The ego is not involved at all, and the energy is very high-frequency. When you're open on that channel, the transmissions manifest more easily. The energy is traveling in both directions between you and the divine. It's a conversation."

A friend of mine said to me recently, "I can't afford to pay my rent and I'm overwhelmed by all my problems. I'm not manifesting very well."

But after some discussion she began to see that she was, in fact, manifesting perfectly, and that her soul was creating lessons through chaos and poverty instead of abundance and peace, because these things were needed for her growth at the time. It was a big revelation for her (and the following week she found a job).

When it appears that we're not getting exactly what we want, it's because we're not on the Gratitude Channel. If we were, we'd see that we're getting exactly what our *souls* seek and create, which doesn't necessarily match up with what our *egos* seek and create. On the Gratitude

Channel, when your dog gets hit by a truck you can say to yourself, "This a moment I created for a purpose that I may not be able to see yet, but it's clearly part of a growth plan that I designed before I came into this incarnation." That's how you start to see the connection between thought and matter. Until you activate that opening you will feel victimized -- rather than in control of -- your creations.

So how do we activate that opening?

Meditation and prayer.

8. Prayer, Meditation and Manifestation

"If you bring forth what is within you, what you bring forth will save you. If you withhold what is within you, what you withhold will destroy you."

The Gnostic Gospels

"Meditation is a lot like dying, and the yogis are right about the sacredness of breath. Breath is a bridge between the physical and the non-physical, and the more 'ventilated' you become, the more light you transfer between yourself and Heaven, like bouncing a ball back and forth. We are creation machines that operate on both physical and non-physical systems, and meditation is a bridge between the two. The reason people breathe fewer respirations per minute when they're dying is because they're not sucking as much energy from the physical and they don't need that conduit anymore. They're switching over to a different source of sustenance where they slowly begin to breathe the light of Heaven. Meditation is like that too. The idea is to release as much of your grip on the physical as possible and allow yourself to be moved somewhere else, where you can receive information from another realm of teachers. You don't have to sit up straight, and it doesn't require a lot of training or discipline. Fetal position works just as well as Lotus position, and it's even OK if you fall asleep, because you'll receive information in your dreams if you ask for it."

Danny

DECODING YOUR INTERNAL DIALOG

The term "internal dialog" describes the relentless babble that goes on in your mind during all your waking hours. We all know what it is, and most of us dismiss it as a psychological clearinghouse of random ideas and images that aren't worth much because we can never seem to grab onto one and actually *do something with it.*

Contrary to what I'd heard about Buddhist meditation techniques where we're supposed to empty our minds (impossible!), as I studied channeling I learned a whole new style of meditating which has to do with allowing the cosmic debris and internal dialog to flow rather than attempting to stifle it. As I practiced this I noticed that messages began to emerge from within these frenetic scenes. In the middle of running a constant stream of junk through my mind—the grocery list, my relationship issues, reminders to put air in the tires of my car—a variety of unexpected images and vignettes would appear. As I became more relaxed and more trusting in the divine, I found I could latch on to a particular scene and hold it for a microsecond longer than the others, thereby releasing the others and retaining the ones that caught my interest.

As I honed this skill, I found I could not only hold a scene, but also travel deeper into it, to a point where fresh, related thoughts and visions would spin off from the original one. With practice, I learned to follow this progression of thoughts, one leading into another, slowing the process just enough to identify hidden messages in the endless parade of images. It's almost a semi-dream state, similar to what you experience just before you fall asleep or wake up (and in fact, it's perfectly OK to fall asleep while you're doing this because messages are also transmitted through dreams).

Within these "debris streams" I hear words or complete thoughts, and it's this very mechanism that allows me to hear Danny and his friends. For most people in an ordinary state of consciousness, these things whiz by so fast that we don't hear them. Sometimes we have a sense of something fleeting having been there, but it passes so quickly that we can't focus on it, and even if we can, we don't give it much credence. For me, true meditation is about slowing down the process enough to view each scene long enough to retain it, almost like running a movie in slow motion. I learned that I could ask God, guides and angels for help reading these messages, and I realized that what I was doing by asking for help was, in essence, *praying*.

It's about listening closely to your internal dialog and searching for hidden jewels within it rather that trying to silence it. And when you need help, all you have to do is ask for it. When I began practicing this type of meditation I was astonished at what I found, and in this chapter I want to share with you the things that Danny and my guides have taught me about how to use meditation as a tool for creating balance and well being in your physical and spiritual life.

I'm going to begin by describing what my own internal dialog usually looks like, and I think you'll find that it's not very different from yours. These chatty little gab sessions tend to happen most often when:

1. I'm taking a walk.
2. I can't fall asleep at night.
3. I wake up in the middle of the night and can't get back to sleep.

Sound familiar? Here's what it sounds like (in this case when I'm out hiking with Henry):

What a gorgeous day, wow, the air smells so good. The snow's melting. It's too hot for this jacket, maybe I'll hang it on a tree but someone might come by and steal it. Henry sure is a happy dog, he runs so fast, what if he trips over a gopher hole and breaks a leg? I'm so happy I found this steep hill to hike on, it's really firming up my butt. Jack loved my butt. I can't fit into my size 8 jeans anymore. Oh well, so I'm a size 9 instead of an 8, big deal, why would I complain about something like that? Jeeeezzzz, I'm so vain! I ate too much yesterday, I really need to fart. Aaaahhh, that's better. Where's Henry? Wow, look how blue that sky is! Jack never really loved me. If I get that new client I might be able to save enough for a down payment on a house. Or should I use that money to self-publish my book? That's an interesting idea. I wonder if Jack will ever read my book. My feet hurt. I wonder if I should get some special shoes for the square dancing class. Do ballet slippers have arches? People wear cowboy boots when they square dance, don't they? I need to call my mom today. I wonder if Andrew's OK. I should call Rebecca. I need to fart again. Aaaahhh, that's better. I'm hungry. I'm almost out of shampoo. What time is it? My feet hurt. Where's Henry? I should stop at the store and get some asparagus. I don't eat enough vegetables. I hope I don't forget the shampoo. I feel fat. I wonder if it will snow tomorrow.

What you just read is expressed here at about probably 1/1000th of the speed at which it actually happens. But I think you get the picture. We all do this, and we do it all the time. Many eastern spiritual traditions teach that the goal of meditation is to slow this down to the point where it's completely silent and we go into utter stillness. I don't agree with that at all. In fact, the only time I've ever been able to quiet my mind to any point resembling stillness was during 50 seconds of freefall during my brief flirtation with skydiving.

There are jeweled messages hidden within our rambling internal diatribes, and the goal is to slow them down enough to decode their secrets. Rebecca once described this as a type of debris similar to what you find when you turn on the faucet in a house that's been unoccupied for a while. The water comes out brown for a few seconds, clearing out the rust, minerals and other junk that's accumulated since the last time the faucet was turned on, and eventually the water runs clear. I love this analogy.

I call myself a meditation teacher but admit that I never apprenticed with Suzuki Roshi or spent any time in an ashram or monastery. Even though I've studied many Buddhist teachings, I never quite understood meditation they way they described it, and it wasn't until I was in my early 50s that I began to learn some meditation techniques that actually worked for me. I ended up developing my own system and style, helped along by guides and non-physical teachers, including Danny. It was, for me, all about listening to the voices of teachers in spirit, which can sometimes be quite loud and at other times appear as barely perceptible symbols, triggers and codes.

To illustrate how these hidden messages appear, let's look back at my internal dialog sample. You'll notice that one of the thoughts was *"Do ballet slippers have arches?"* Ballet has zero significance in my life, yet there they were, pink satin ballet slippers in the middle of a rapid-fire sequence of thoughts about square dancing. While it might seem like a logical segue related to dancing, for some reason this thought stood out as different from others, and beckoned me to follow it. Its purpose, I realize now, was to serve as a teaching aid for this chapter, so that I could make a point about how listening to these thoughts can help you manifest specific actions in physical reality.

Here's how it works...

In a high-speed panorama of ten thousand seemingly unrelated thoughts, an image of ballet slippers flashes past. You don't even notice it, and even if you do, it's instantly forgotten. Two weeks later a friend shows up with an extra ticket to the ballet and asks you to come along because her intended companion had to bow out at the last minute. You're not really interested in ballet and can't think of a more boring way to spend an evening, but for some reason, although it's completely out of character for you to attend a ballet, you agree to go. During the intermission you meet someone at the lobby bar who turns out to be the love of your life. Of course you have no recollection of the fleeting image of ballet slippers that popped into your consciousness two weeks earlier.

My personal meditation practice is about seeking and remembering these types of images, because they are messages from angels and guides. Stopping and focusing on a specific thought or image is not as difficult as it seems. Keep a notebook or voice recorder handy anytime you're in a meditative state (during meditation, while drifting off to sleep, when you're dreaming or when you're in any sort of quiet space). Jot down or record any thoughts or images that catch your attention, regardless of how "meaningless" they seem to be. After a while you'll have a meditation journal that will amaze you when you look back at it, and you'll begin to see the links and patterns that emerge. You'll notice how these messages suggest changes in attitudes or activities, and even hint at future experiences. This is how you begin the process of listening to divine guidance, and it's the first step toward manifesting changes in your reality.

This is what Danny means when he talks about the Inter-dimensional Postal Service (IPS). The United Parcel Service (UPS) delivers packages to people. But these are *psychic* packages, delivered on time, every time, between dimensions. When I first heard this phrase from Danny -- as I was falling asleep one night -- I scribbled it down in my meditation journal, but had no recollection of it the next morning. I didn't find it until I looked at my journal a few days later. What a huge loss it would have been to let that one get away!

Meditation has become my greatest pleasure, and I find myself going deeper all the time. In the process, my judgments about everything, including religion, fall away. I've even started studying the works of Teresa of Avila, an early Christian mystic who traveled extensively through other realms, reporting back to us in poetic language that describes the meditation journey in beautiful detail. Years ago I would never have read anything even remotely related to the Catholic church. Now I find some of the ancient practices and rituals of early Christianity, Islam and other western religious traditions extremely appealing, just as Arlen predicted.

Like many people, I recoil from religious structure, dogma and the concept of a judgmental god. However, blatant rejection can cause us to throw the baby out with the bathwater and end up rejecting *spirituality*, which has nothing at all to do with religion. Through learning to meditate I began to see, without any doubt, that divine energy *does* exist, and in the process, I slowly allowed certain words into my vocabulary that I'd declared moratoriums on for decades, such as *prayer*, *angels and God.* The more I meditated, the more my resistance to the idea of divine energy began to transform and I could soon use these words comfortably in my conversations.

This was an unexpected turn of events for me. There was a time in my life when I was very active on the board of directors of the American Humanist Association, an organization that rejects metaphysics and spirituality completely. I was even ordained as a Humanist minister, which loosely implies an atheistic, skeptical or agnostic perspective, though arguably this is open to interpretation. Although I worked within these parameters, I embraced many metaphysical ideas but kept them to myself when mingling in Humanist circles. When the Humanist Association heard that I was writing this book, the president called and politely asked me to resign. I now *proudly* refer to myself as an "excommunicated Humanist and defrocked Humanist minister."

THE SATELITTE DISCOVERY

Speaking of the traditional interpretation of religious ideas, I came up with a way to explain my idea of prayer by using what I call "the Satellite Discovery." I figured this out one night when Danny was about 11 years old and having trouble falling asleep. We both had to get up at 6 am for school in the morning, and I could hear him tossing and turning in his room through the baby monitor. By 11:30 pm I was desperate for him to fall asleep, and I said out loud, "please God, let him sleep."

The moment I said that I had to laugh at the absurdity of asking a third party for intervention. I was lying in my bed and Danny was in his bed in the next room, separated from me by a wall. But here I was sending a request to some remote location in the universe where some esoteric idea called "God" would hear my request and beam down some magic sleeping dust to help Danny sleep. It was as if I were sending a message to a satellite in space that would somehow be able to send signals to Danny's brain to make him sleep. Seems like a complicated, long distance system for doing something I could probably do just as well without a middleman. So I tried it.

I started breathing deeply with an intentional, even rhythm, sending this rhythm to Danny's breaths as I heard them through the monitor. With each breath I imagined Danny covered in soothing pink light, and synchronized his breathing with mine until he was in a slower, more restful state. I sent messages to his mind saying, "You can relax now, you can let go and fall into a safe, comfortable sleep. There's nothing you need to do, your body is done with its work for today, and you can let go and float away into sleep."

Within about two minutes I could hear his breathing slowing down (I had to fight to keep myself awake because the exercise was relaxing me as well). He was soon sound asleep, but I was suddenly wide awake, excited about my discovery that God is NOT a satellite orbiting the earth beaming secret messages to selected receivers. Instead, I learned, *we can beam the messages directly to each other and to ourselves!* The satellite is merely a source of energy and power for us to draw upon, but we have to do the actual work ourselves. God is an energy source, and we work in partnership with that source.

As Danny regularly reminds me, God functions like a pilot light, a force that energizes everything and keeps us connected to it because *we are part of it*, temporarily split off into physical forms on earth. In this sense we can truly be called God's "children." We can ask God to help us by sending more energy by supercharging our own light and raising our vibrational frequencies so that we can become more aligned with the source and hence more receptive to the collective power.

This is always available to us, *if we ask*. In this way, we don't have to ask the pilot light to heal someone; we merely have to strengthen our connection to it in order to transmit healing energy using our own healing powers. I could put Danny to sleep just by harnessing some of that energy and directing it toward his body. If I could put someone to sleep, I could certainly heal someone, if the intention of that person's soul is to be healed (more about healing can be found in Chapter 10).

A FEW SAMPLE MEDITATIONS

In this chapter I'm going to introduce you to specific meditations that I learned from Danny, Elishevaa and a handful of other teachers, and also a few that I made up myself. While it's certainly helpful to get yourself into a quiet state by lighting a candle and doing some deep breathing, it's not always necessary; some of these can be done while driving your car or waiting in line at the bank. But I don't want to discount the importance of proper breathing to help you shift your focus to higher dimensions, so here's a quick lesson on "belly breathing," a common and effective relaxation technique used in hypnotherapy, yoga and meditation.

Inhale deeply, through your nose, so that your stomach -- not your chest -- expands on the inhale (this is the opposite of how we normally breathe, and the more distended and unflattering your stomach looks when you do it, the better). Hold that breath in for a few seconds, as long as it's comfortable, and then blow it out forcefully through your mouth, like you're blowing out candles on a birthday cake. Do these three or four times. As you proceed in your meditation, if you find yourself getting distracted and your thoughts are running wild, simply return to this breathing technique and it will help you to re-focus.

Regarding candles, I love meditating with candles. Candle flames are *light*, and hence they are symbolic of THE light. I also believe that angels and guides are attracted to the light from candles, so use candles whenever you can. Music is also useful, depending on the meditation and your ability to concentrate. I find some music distracting, while other music opens my heart and leaves me weeping in surrender. Try various things until you find what works for you. There are no rules.

I have long since given up the idea that problems can be solved by human interaction or intervention alone. I used to think that if people just communicated honestly enough they could work through anything, but I know now that communication and problem-solving strategies on the earth plane only address half the equation. The rest of it has to be done within one's relationship with one's own soul. That's why meditation and manifestation go hand-in-hand. Wherever you focus your intention is where change will happen, whether it's healing a personal relationship or a blessing for world peace.

Following are descriptions of some of my favorite meditations, and not all of them are the "decoding your internal dialog" type. Some require intense concentration and others are best practiced in a group with a guide. I threw them all into the mix here. Feel free to share them and teach them as you see fit.

The Forgiveness Fly-By

Elishevaa gave this meditation to me and it was the first one I ever tried. If there's someone in your life whom you love but cannot truly love because of anger and pain, this meditation can help you release and forgive, and can do a lot to heal the relationship. It doesn't change the other person, but it can change the way you *react* to that person, and *that* will change the dynamic between you. Releasing the judgments, injuries and fibers that hold you in a dance of sadness and pain with that person is miraculously healing, and at deeper levels of understanding, meditations like this can actually change the way the other person feels (because all communication and all interactions are happening on a soul level). This is an easy and ideal meditation for beginners:

> Think of someone with whom you're in conflict. Picture him wherever you think he might be at the moment, sleeping in his bed, driving his car, working or doing anything that he typically does. He might be in the next room making coffee, or on an airplane flying to another country. It doesn't matter where his body is located in physical space, because you will be working directly with his soul and the exact point where it intersects with your own. Now imagine that your soul is going to fly by and visit his. Picture him standing or sitting there, and as you approach, shower him with the sparkling light of forgiveness. Say to yourself, or out loud, *"I forgive you for not doing what I want you to do. I release you from my expectations. I am grateful for what you've taught me in this life. I bless and honor your soul and the path that it's on, and I give you my love from the most divine source within me."* Visualize white, gold or pink light flowing from your heart to his, covering his body and filling the room that he occupies.

> This is extremely difficult to do when you're angry and in the midst of conflict, but that's the best time and the best reason for doing this exercise. You'll see the dynamic between you change *energetically*, because the souls can communicate even when the bodies can't.

Danny's Stardust Meditation for Children

When Danny was 12 years old I decided to teach him how to meditate. I'd guide him through this one when I put him to bed at night, after turning off the lights (he had those glow-in-the-dark plastic stars stuck to his ceiling and they shined brightly when the lights went off). This is a beautiful meditation for children of any age, with or without the plastic stars. I'd lie down next to him and after looking at the stars for a few minutes I'd say, very slowly and gently:

111

Close your eyes and breathe very slowly for a few seconds. I'm going to count each breath you take, ready? One... two... three. Now imagine that every time you breathe in you are inhaling zillions of tiny stars of all different colors, like rainbow stardust. Every time you inhale, the stars go inside you and fill you up with beautiful, colored light. And when you exhale, you blow them all out again. Breathe them in, hold them inside you for a few seconds, and then blow them out. This is what energy looks like, and it's the energy of everything in creation. It's the energy of all the people you love, and the energy of dogs and trees and rocks and planets and feelings and ideas and bodies and spirits and everything. As you breathe this energy in and out you will know that you're connected to this energy all the time, and that you can never be separated from it, no matter what. And you can never be separated from anybody else either, because we're all made of this same stardust. It's the stuff that connects us, whether we're alive or dead. This is what God is. This is what love is.

Danny *loved* this. He did his best to keep his eyes closed (his neurological problems made it difficult for him to keep his eyes voluntarily closed), but he'd always smile and giggle as we walked through this meditation. It was one of the ways in which I prepared him for the idea that he would be leaving physical life in a few years. I wanted him to know that we would not be separate after death. Sometimes I think he was giggling because he knew far more about this stuff than I did and he was amused at my feeble attempts to explain it.

Asking a Guide for Healing

The basis for this meditation was taught to me at the 2006 Sand, Sea & Spirit conference by a woman named Carolyn Weislogel, and it's a beautiful exercise in learning to trust spirit. I've added a few of my own touches to it, and as is true for most of the meditations in this chapter, they are best when guided. If you have nobody to guide you, read them out loud into a tape recorder and listen to the tape whenever you need to be walked through the meditation. Remember to leave brief pauses between each step to allow yourself some time to stay in those moments. The guiding voice should always be soft, slow and soothing:

Imagine you see a beautiful meadow or field in front of you. It can be any kind of field... green, grassy, desert, shoreline, whatever you like. Now begin to move across the field slowly, enjoying its beauty, its fragrance and anything else you perceive there. At the end of the field you see a rainbow, and you are going to walk through it, from one color to another, walking through one color at a time, as if you're walking through a hallway made of each color. Begin by walking through the red, and then gradually let it turn to orange as you continue to walk slowly through. Next you'll come to yellow, and as you pass thorough you'll see green in the distance. Walk through the green and notice that it begins changing into light blue. The light blue becomes darker until you're walking through a beautiful cobalt blue, and then finally, deep purple before you emerge back out into the light of day (note: in walking through each of these colors you are clearing each of your chakras).

When you come out of the rainbow you see a lush, green garden, full of vines, flowers and soft grasses. As you approach you'll notice that someone is standing there. It can be a human or an animal, male or female, or it can have no form at all, appearing as only energy. This is a guide, a being of light. Go to the guide and simply be with it for several seconds. There's no need for introductions or words. If the guide speaks to you that's wonderful, but it isn't necessary. Just *be*. Tell the guide that you want to do some healing work, and ask it to give you access to light, energy and wisdom to help you do this work. Also ask for help in believing without question that you can access this place, this guide and this energy any time you like.

You may stay with this guide as long as you wish. Ask for pictures of areas in your life that need healing. Then visualize those pictures floating away and being transmuted into light. You can also give this guide a basket containing anything you wish to release, such as addictions, negative attachments, fears, doubts, a particular relationship or anything that comes to mind. The guide will take these things and transmute them into light.

Visiting the Chakras

The basis for this one can be found in Doreen Virtue 's book *Chakra Clearing*. I've altered it a bit, and even if you don't understand very much about the chakras, this exercise will still be effective (it may also inspire you to learn more about chakras and how to work with them).

In this meditation you will "visit" each chakra, taking note of the images it sends to you and listening to its messages. When you sense pain or imbalance, you'll focus healing light into that chakra. This is a very powerful meditation. A lot of deep work can be done here. I suggest you keep pen and paper handy (or your voice recorder) and write down your impressions as you visit each chakra:

Begin by imagining your root chakra, which is located at the base of your spine, as a red ball or orb, radiating with energy. This chakra represents the most basic elements of your existence and the survival of your physical body. Any issues you have regarding health, security, money, shelter and your physical existence in general are carried in the first chakra. Ask this chakra to communicate with you. What thoughts, fears and images come up? Allow these images to come through, and with each one that has fear or doubt attached to it, say this little prayer: *"I release my fears and doubts about survival. I put my absolute trust in spirit and know that I am safe and have everything I need."* Envision the negative images floating away and disappearing as the red color of the chakra becomes stronger and more vibrant.

Now visit your second chakra, which radiates with the color orange (you can visualize it as a ball or orb, or just visualize the color itself in no particular form). It's located in your pelvic area and is related to your creative expressions; what you originate and express to the world. This includes procreation and the formation of relationships and children, which is why it also represents sexuality and sexual energy. Visit this chakra now and ask it to show you what's going on in your soul energetically where creation, sex and relationship is concerned. What kind of images do you see? Are you feeling peace or fear? Is there a relationship that needs to heal or to move forward in some way? Listen to what this chakra is telling you, and say these words, *"I release my fears about relationship and my creations. I open myself up to sexual health and relatedness. I put my absolute trust in spirit and know that I am whole and loved."* Envision the negative images floating away and disappearing as the orange color of the chakra becomes more radiant and vibrant.

The third chakra is yellow and is located in your solar plexus. This is the source of your personal power; spiritual, emotional, physical and intellectual. It's also the place where your control issues can be found. Look at this chakra to see if there are places in you where your power is being compromised, suppressed or perhaps even abused. Allow the power to live and breathe inside you. Ask it what it needs. Heal the places in which your power may be dimming or overshadowed by fear, or places in which your power may be channeled in unhealthy ways. Say this prayer: *"I breathe life into my personal power. I choose to follow my truth and know that I am connected to divine power at all times. I release my need to control outcomes and other people, and I put my complete faith in the light of love."* Visualize the yellow color glowing like the sun inside you.

The fourth chakra is the energy of the heart, which for many people needs the most healing. The color is green. The heart is your center, exactly at the center of the seven chakras. Put your hands on your chest and feel your heart. Ask it what it needs and where it hurts, and allow it to express itself to you. You may see images of people you love who've hurt you. Release them to the light, forgive them and let them float away. Look at the color of your heart chakra. Is it dull and dirty, covered by the bruises of anger and resentment? Imagine the green color becoming clear like an emerald. Say, *"I release the pain and anger held in my heart. My heart is open and I know that it is safe to love and be loved. My heart is filled with divine love, and my ability to release and forgive is limitless. I no longer need to hold on to pain or injury in this area."*

The next chakra, the fifth, is the throat chakra, and its color is light blue. This is where communication and truth live, and many of us who've been afraid of speaking the truth are very wounded here. Breathe deeply as you examine the fifth chakra and ask it what it needs to say. What images do you see and what words do you hear? Have you been afraid to speak out? Where are the communication obstructions in your life? See this chakra as an infinitely open, clear blue sky, and say, *"I will speak my truth fearlessly. I am wise, and my words and visions have value. I do not need to swallow my words and my feelings. It's safe to communicate without fear or hesitation."*

The sixth chakra, which is a gorgeous, deep cobalt blue, creates a bridge between the physical and non-physical worlds. This is where manifestation happens. This is where thought becomes matter. It's located around the area of your "third eye," in the middle of your forehead. At this level you can become aware of how you've used the power in all the other chakras to create your reality. What are you manifesting? What are you bringing into your life? Is your ego in charge or are you listening to Spirit? Ask this chakra, in prayer, to help you open up to divine messages, by saying, "I understand that my thoughts create my reality. I choose to work in union with God and my guides to manifest what is highest and best for my soul."

Finally we arrive at the seventh chakra, which is your launching pad to Heaven. It is at the top of your head and is known as the "crown chakra." This is where you recognize that everything in the universe is connected. This is where you know that you are ONE with everything. This is where you completely let go and merge into the divine ocean. This is the will of God, which is no different than the intention of your own soul. The prayer is, "I surrender my ego, my judgments and my resistance. I release my fears. I want only truth. I surrender to God."

This is very powerful work. It *will* change your life.

The Duality Meditation

This one is an imaginative hybrid of Danny's Stardust Meditation and the Forgiveness Fly-by, but much more advanced and on a much grander scale. I saved it for the end of this chapter because it's very heavy, a little longer than then others, and extremely potent. It takes you beyond your own self and shows you how deeply you are connected to other people and the universe. I've led this meditation for groups many times and it

116

brings people to tears. It's extremely transformative because it opens the heart and helps us see how we're connected to one another by showing us the divinity in all things. It's a long one; about seven minutes, and is best done with a facilitator who can slowly, gently walk you through it. It begins with imagining the same multi-colored stars from Danny's stardust meditation:

Begin by taking slow belly breaths until you feel yourself calming and separating from the cares of the day. When you can focus, start imagining a field of billions of sparkling stars, but instead of white stars, see them in colors... billions of multi-colored stars against either a background of dark night or a white background, whichever is easiest for you to visualize. It is a living, radiant field of colorful stardust, and with each breath, you inhale this magical stardust, which is the divine light of the universe filling your body and aligning you with the pure energy of creation.

As you exhale, release the stardust and give that light to the world around you. Inhale the field of stars deeply, letting them fill you with light. And then exhale them and return them to the field. You are breathing pure light, which contains every color in the spectrum and can be any color you choose. Whatever color comes to you, receive it without question. Take a few seconds to breathe it in and out.

Now imagine someone you love, and exhale the starlight out onto that person, covering him or her with this light. This light is your LOVE, and you're sharing it with this person, telling him or her that you forgive her for any pain that's existed between you. You are releasing this person -- and yourself -- from that pain. In a state of love like this, there is no judgment, no blame, only the love that connects us all, the material from which we are all made. The love that is God, represented by the starlight you are sharing right now.

Now imagine someone else, this time a stranger, someone different from you, someone with whom you would not typically identify. Perhaps it's a woman with a baby in a famine-ravaged country. She is suffering, but you can focus your starlight onto her and lift her up with your love, breathing life and hope into her heart. You are not separate from her. You are made of the same light and you are as connected to her as you are to your own parents, spouse or children. The starlight binds you and wraps its love around you. You are a conduit for this love. You can heal with the light you send.

Now envision another stranger, perhaps this time a businessman on Wall Street or a senator in Washington DC. Shower him with your light, breathe stardust onto him, bring him into the same oneness that includes the woman with the baby and the loved one you envisioned earlier. Cover this man with the same starlight that is yours to share, and bring him into your realm of healing. And while you're at it, bring in all the other people walking next to him, all of New York, all of America, millions of people brought into the oneness that you are now becoming aware of. This is the love we are all made of. This is God. We all have this inside us.

Now expand your healing light to include people on earth that you judge as bad or evil, like an abusive parent or partner that you can't forgive. Perhaps you see someone like Sadaam Hussein or Hitler. Know that these people are desperately in need of healing love. They are made of the same light that you're breathing and sharing now. Cover them with this light, just as you would for your dearest friend. Remember that we are all *one*. We are each other's creations.

Now step back from these people, these individuals, and look at all the beings on the planet, the people, the animals, the trees, the water and the insects, the entire beautiful planet itself, and everybody on it, whether you see them as good or bad. Wrap the entire planet in the light of this sacred love.

Now step back a bit further and expand your view to include other planets and their inhabitants, other bodies in space, and everything else in the Universe. Bring it all into your breath and your light. And know that THIS is God. Breathe into that idea for a few seconds.

And now you will start to notice that you've returned to your starting point, to the field of stars from which you first drew this light with your first breath in this meditation. In a sense you've returned to your first breath of life in a human body and the first breath of light that created the universe. You've returned HOME. Be with that for a little while, breathe it in and out, and then slowly come back to your body, and open your eyes whenever you're ready.

I Release My Fear and Anger Into The Light

In contrast to the last meditation, this one is quick and simple. Whenever you're stressed or depressed, if you're panicking or angry or feeling completely out of control, simply light a candle and repeat these words until you are calm: *"I release my fear and anger into the light. I release my fear and anger into the light..."* This will summon the angels and guides to help you to become calm. It's a great one to do while stuck in a traffic jam (but without the candle, or you may get to Heaven sooner than you think).

DANNY ON MEDITATION

Now that we've examined some meditations and techniques, here are a few excerpts from conversations I've had with Danny about meditation and connecting to spirit in general:

ME: I love the idea of "ventilating" ourselves with light and breath. Tell me more about this.

DAN: Ventilation lightens the body; it diffuses matter, returns matter to a vibrational state, almost like traveling backwards in manifestation. These vibrations make energy denser, and that energy can ultimately become dense enough to create matter. Meditation reverses that process. It makes the energy less dense and releases us from matter by ventilating us with light and higher frequencies, releasing us from the grip of the body. The same sort of thing happens when you die, except you release from the body completely rather than partially. You're able to do this because the consciousness knows that it's finished with its work in that particular body. In dream states and meditation states, while the body is still alive, the consciousness knows that it's not done yet, so it continues to do its work while still being part of the body.

ME: What does this have to do with auras?

DAN: Auras are energy fields to which you can "lift" yourself into a more ventilated state. They're the ventilated version of yourself. When you transcend matter, you move into the auric body through the "holes" created by ventilation. So you can be almost completely in your aura and not in your body at all while in these other states. The auric body is on a higher frequency so it can communicate with other dimensions more easily.

ME: Why is it so hard to meditate and communicate with other realms when there's strong emotion present?

DAN: Anxiety is usually about fear, and fear is a very low frequency. In intense fear you are afraid that you'll lose everything, that you'll be annihilated, and in fact, you will be. Your ego will be annihilated; it will dissolve so that the truth of your soul can come forth. If you walk through your fear, walk right into the face of the things that scare you the most, you will raise your vibration and your Higher Self will speak clearly. Symbols and rituals can help. Anything that bridges the gap between the ego and the soul will take you higher. Remember what you did with the chakra cups? Everything you asked for came true. You were in the middle of intense fear at that time, but you used symbols to express what your soul needed, and it helped move your fear out of the way.[3]

When in doubt, when you're emotionally distraught and can't connect, simply pray for divine love to reach you. This is what Jesus meant when he said "I am the way and the light." He is a representative of the light, and he's teaching that the way to peace is through blending with higher frequencies. Peace can never be found inside the mind or the ego, or in trying to fix or control a situation. It can only be found through your connection to Spirit. To live without this connection is not living. I'm helping you right now because we

---

[3] During the months following Danny's death, when I was making plans to leave my marriage, I was in a state of panic every day. One day in a store I found a set of little glass candle holders in the colors of the chakras. I bought them, set them up on an altar and put objects representing each chakra's energy into the appropriate cup. For example, in the red cup representing the first chakra (physical survival, money) I put a dollar. In the green cup representing the heart chakra, I put a little stone with the word "gratitude" painted on it. In the light blue cup, representing communication, I put some coins and some scraps of paper with excerpts from this book representing my intention to publish these words.

have an agreement to do this work together, but you don't really need me or Jesus or anybody, because you can align with those forces on your own. When you do, you will have the same gifts that Jesus and all the great teachers have. Those gifts are available to everybody. The teachers are merely emissaries.

ME: So that's how prayer works? One just asks for alignment and the intention of the soul will become clear?

DAN: Yes, that's the true function of prayer, to open you up to divine energy so your Higher Self can be heard. Every time you go to your special place by the river to pray, the conduit between you and Heaven opens up more easily. Of course it isn't necessary to go to the river; we can always hear you no matter where you are. But the fact that you made a conscious effort to create a symbolic place, just like you did with the chakra cups, helps to raise your frequency so that it's easier for *you* to hear *us*. Symbols are very helpful, which is why there is so much symbolism and ritual in the world's religions. Symbols and rituals help you focus on Spirit because they give your intention a physical form. They bridge the gap between the realms.

When you did your Mother's Day ritual you were very sad.[4] You knew you were stuck behind a membrane of grief and anger and you needed to break through it. You also knew that these emotions were keeping you from meditating effectively, and once you faced that and worked with it through prayer and ritual, the channel opened up again. You are beginning to understand how sadness blocks the flow of communication from Heaven, but at the same time, you're not supposed to deny your sadness. On the contrary, you're supposed to walk through it in excruciating detail. In prayer you don't ask for your sadness to disappear. You ask to see it and understand it more clearly, to process it and feel it until balance is established. Most people just find ways to cover up their pain or to make it "go away,"

---

[4] My cabin in Oregon was on a bluff overlooking a river. I found a beautiful spot by the river and I built a "medicine wheel" there, where I did many ceremonies and meditations. On Mothers Day 2007 I did a ceremony honoring my life as Danny's mother. I brought pictures of him and other scared objects, and I thanked Spirit for giving me this beautiful boy and for the inter-dimensional relationship we now share. I also used this ritual to help me release Jack, and tossed my wedding ring into the river to symbolize my pain, attachment and anger being washed away by the water.

but of course it never just goes away. It needs to be faced and processed and *consciously* made part of your growth.

Human emotions exist for a reason. They irritate you like a speck of dirt irritates the inside of an oyster to make a pearl. This is why you can't talk to Heaven 24 hours a day. Sometimes you have to disconnect so that you can experience the human emotions that propel you toward connection. When you realize that every thought is a prayer, then you'll know that prayer is always answered.

9. Grief, Guilt and What it's Like To Die

"Of course I didn't die ... nobody dies."

Danny

At this writing I'm in the midst of a crippling, guilt-filled depression about Danny's final days, crying almost hourly and feeling as if I'd done something wrong somewhere along the way, as if something important is missing, perhaps a lack in my awareness or a skipped step that would be vital to my grieving process. I don't know what it is, but it's been keeping me agitated, edgy and unable to concentrate on work or simple tasks.

I'd learned from Danny, Arlen, Elishevaa and others that when in emotional pain, the only source of comfort comes from Spirit. But it's difficult to connect with God, Spirit or the Higher Self when there's so much emotion and fear present. Yet it's that very emotion that gets our attention and leads us to divine guidance. When we feel lost, afraid, overwhelmed or uncertain, it's because messages are trying to come through and we're not hearing them. As Danny once explained, "it's your psychic cell phone ringing."

This chapter is the answer to the ringing of my psychic cell phone. The anxiety I've been feeling is a *call to action.* When I pray and call out for relief, I get this consistent message: *stop everything and work on the book.* Writing is an ideal channel for giving your guides a voice. Even if you're not writing a book or you think you can't write, you can accomplish the same thing by simply keeping a journal. Just start writing and trust what comes out. Eventually you will see that information is coming from Spirit.

THE ANAMCARA PROJECT

Before I share what Danny has told me about illness, death and grief, I must first share a quick story that illustrates how we are led by

123

unseen forces, in conjunction with our own souls, to exactly where we're supposed to be.

When I moved to Oregon I was in a state of chaos, having just experienced Danny's death and the end of a marriage. I was eager to start my life over, and, miraculously, some opportunities arose that provided me with new friends and an affordable, beautiful place to live. These things just fell into my lap, and the whole plan came together quite conveniently. This was the reason I chose Central Oregon.

Or so I thought.

One of the first things I did when I arrived in Oregon was to sign up as a hospice volunteer. Ever since Danny's death and our subsequent communication through the IPS, I'd become interested in working with people who are dying. Via a referral from the local hospice, I was introduced to a program called "The Anamcara Project." I'd never heard this strange word before, but learned that it's a Gaelic term referring to someone who acts as a "soul friend to the dying." In ancient Celtic traditions, helping to guide people's souls into the next world was equal to being a midwife who guides new babies into *this* world. Interestingly, Elishevaa had used the word "midwife" when helping me prepare for Danny's death. It makes perfect sense, because death is not the opposite of life. It's the opposite of birth.

The Anamcara Project is run by a remarkable couple named Richard and Mary Groves. Richard is a former Catholic priest and a brilliant religious scholar who travels the world with Mary studying death traditions and practices from different cultures and religions. Their work is supported by an advisory board of world-famous spiritual teachers, religious leaders, healers, writers, social scientists and metaphysicians. The two-year Anamcara training program teaches students how to work with the souls of dying people to help heal any issues that may be keeping them from having a peaceful death. It incorporates teachings, music, prayer and ritual from many different faith traditions, including Buddhist, Christian, Hebrew, Islamic, Shamanistic and Celtic.

When I realized that Richard and Mary's group was based right here in Central Oregon and that the training sessions were held at a location *five minutes from my house,* I knew at once that this was the real reason I came here. I was divinely directed, and everything clicked into place when I realized this. I'm now enrolled in the Anamcara project and it's become more important to me than I can possibly describe. And to my surprise and delight, it turns out that my buddy Carolyn Myss is involved with the group. The signs are loud and clear.

One of the training sessions included a presentation by a woman named Gail Coon, a harpist and hospice volunteer who visits people during the last days of their lives and plays soothing music for them. In this presentation she talked about how *hearing* is the last sense to disappear as the body shuts down, and she played beautiful melodies to illustrate how the various musical modes correspond to the chakras and how important it is for the dying to hear peaceful sounds.

I wasn't prepared for how acutely her presentation would touch on the deep guilt I feel about the sounds that were in Danny's environment during his final days. The day before Danny died, while he lay on the couch struggling to breathe, I went to give him his medicine and Jack flew into a rage, screaming at me about "fussing over Danny too much." He ranted for 20 minutes while Nicole and I sobbed and pleaded with him to stop acting that way in front of Danny. But he didn't stop, and in fact got louder and meaner by the minute, until Nicole and I actually left the house, thinking it was the best way to get him to stop. This was by far the worst moment of my entire life, and even though Danny has reassured me about it a hundred times since he died, I can't imagine ever being able to get over the guilt I carry about that day.

I got so upset during Gail's presentation that I had to flee from the room. I couldn't stop crying and had a sudden onset of stomach cramps and diarrhea, which gave me a good excuse to spend the next 15 minutes in the bathroom where I'd have some privacy to cry my heart out. I had a very hard time gaining my composure and realized that I wasn't going to be able to get through this alone. I waited until Gail's presentation was over and then reached out to a woman I'd met earlier who was a grief counselor (most of the people in the program are hospice nurses, chaplains or therapists). She listened to me and helped me work through my feelings, assuring me that lots of people fall apart like this during Anamcara trainings because learning to deal with our own grief and guilt is part of the process. How else would we be able to help others who are grieving?

When I got home that evening and was sitting on my deck watching the sun set over the river, I asked Danny, "What kind of Anamcara can I be if I didn't do right by my own son? How can I help people when my own guilt is so crippling?" And he said:

125

"This is exactly what you're supposed to be working on right now, and it is part of your Anamcara training. If you hadn't experienced this guilt you would not be able to help others when they experience it. In many ways the guilt can be seen as a gift. Aspects of your guilt are necessary for your compassion in working with dying people and their families. By way of my death, I handed you a sacred scepter to carry forward. You learned something from my death that you can now take to another's.

We all live the same life and die the same death and breathe the same breath. It never stops or starts, begins or ends, it's one breath, one movement, one organism. As the Course in Miracles says, 'there's only one of us here.' Your work is my work. There's no difference between us. The two of us are one pulsing light in terms of this work. We're doing it together, and the pain is a required part of the experience and was part of an agreement we made long ago. You would not have the depth and the soul for working with the dying if you weren't in pain right now. You acted as a midwife for my death, helping me move into my new life in Heaven, and I'm now midwifing you into *your* new life.

The pain you're feeling now is humbling you, it's making you wake up, making you feel and making you write about guilt in our book. The pain is doing its job perfectly. I came to you as a child with a life-threatening illness and you took care of me. Now I take care of you, and through that, you will take care of others through writing, teaching and working in the Anamcara tradition. We pass the energy around. We're all one, working together to create growth. There are no tragedies, no coincidences and no accidents."

Danny and I have had several dialogs about what happens when we die, how to deal with grief, and other aspects of illness, disability and death. In this chapter I've taken the information he's given me and categorized it by topics. At times some of it may seem random and unrelated, but it's all quite astonishing any way you look at it.

THE 11TH HOUR

The hours immediately before Danny died were the most profound hours I've ever experienced in my life, and were my motivation for becoming a hospice volunteer and studying Anamcara. Those hours were a *prayer*, a shining spark of sacred purity and honor. I had never felt so connected to spirit as I did that morning, five hours before he died, when I watched him lying there with his eyes open, staring up at the ceiling.

He was looking up, but his eyes were focused a few inches behind his head rather than straight up above him, as I described in Chapter One. It was as if he was watching a movie projected on the ceiling, and as I learned later, this was the period in which he was floating up through the crack in the egg. In my meditations I often lie down in that exact position, with my eyes focused that same way, and when I do, I experience a flood of energy and emotion. It's as if I'm looking through my third eye, and at times it seems I can feel something very close to what Danny must have been feeling during those hallowed hours. Naturally, I asked him to tell me more about this, and this was our conversation:

DAN: I was already out of my body at that time, and I was quite busy, interacting with all kinds of people who'd come to help me. Scientists and doctors like to say that people are 'hallucinating' at this stage, and it makes one wonder, what exactly are hallucinations if not messages from other realms? I knew that I was ready to lose my physical body so I just willed myself to detach from it, and I felt no pain at all. It's true that my eyes were drying up from dehydration and it was difficult to see, but it didn't matter, because there was nothing in the physical world that I needed to see. What I saw instead was internal, in my soul. I saw the bonds to which we are all connected. Please tell this to everyone.

ME: Grandpa's face looked like that when he was dying. Was he out of his body at that time? Do people leave their bodies before they actually die?

DAN: At a certain point the pull from Heaven is so strong and so irresistible that the soul is drawn to it and the pleasure of being pulled in that direction is beyond description. The love of the guides and angels is so powerful that the soul can feast on the beauty of Heaven while the body still breathes. Even while the body still has physical life force running through it, the soul is slowly finding its way home. There is still some intention holding the body, because the time for a body to actually physically die depends on many things. One of these things is the soul agreements of the people around the dying person, such as agreements about who will be present for the last breath, what the dynamics were between family members at that moment and how those dynamics were handled. The experience of

127

the loved ones in that moment has an impact on how they'll feel and what they'll work on for the rest of their lives.

For example, you feel guilty about not playing beautiful music for me as I was dying and not being with me at the moment my body died. But you're learning that it's that same guilt which is propelling you toward a higher level of spiritual study and service. It was our agreement that the details surrounding my last 24 hours on earth would be exactly as they were. The soul stays connected to earth only closely enough to fulfill the agreements about the circumstances surrounding the moment of physical death.

This is why one can never control or choose when another dies and why there should not be any guilt or remorse about the so-called "hastening" of someone's death with the drugs used in hospice care. It is not possible to hasten anything. It's only possible to listen to the person's soul and follow its intention. Everybody is following this, though most are not aware of it. The drugs help the soul to separate, because they slow the body down so much that it doesn't require much input from the soul any more and the body stays alive—just barely—on its own while the soul begins its travels. Just like you can raise or lower the frequency of your energy and consciousness through meditation and breath control, so can the body's frequency be adjusted so that it doesn't require much to stay alive. It no longer requires any of its senses and it barely requires air. The drugs used in hospice care are nothing new. Natural forms of these drugs have been used by ancient people for thousands of years to assist people with their dying.

ME: What about when somebody dies suddenly or violently? Do they leave the body before the body is technically dead?

DAN: Yes, even if there's only a fraction of a second in which it can happen. The death, regardless of how it is brought about, whether one dies in a plane crash or drowns in the bathtub, is part of that person's life plan. Some spiritual teachers believe that the soul knows several days in advance of the body dying, and in many cases this is true. But it is ALWAYS true that the soul knows moments before the body dies, because it is the soul's intention that keeps a body alive. When the intention changes, the soul chooses to be drawn toward Heaven and leaves the body to fend on its own for varying periods of time. My body -- and grandpa's too -- was on autopilot for several hours before it shut down completely. Our souls

128

were already gone. This is why the stories that are told about out-of-body experiences are so validating and so important for research. Some of those experiences happen while the body is still barely alive, and others happen after the body is technically dead. Either way, it's the soul's intention that determines what happens.

ME: Dan, medically speaking, your body starved to death, and there's a lot of political, religious and social controversy about life support, feeding tubes and such. I always worried that you might be hungry, even though your body wasn't able to process food. I made the decision against a feeding tube on my own because you couldn't talk, and I never really knew what *you* would have wanted. Did I "hasten" your death? Were you in pain at all toward the end? The autopsy report said your body weighed 54 pounds when you died. It breaks my heart to think of you like that.

DAN: Silly mom! You know you have no control over when another person dies, as I just explained. And you DO know what I wanted. You knew about my soul's intention on the day I got diagnosed with MLD. But I'm glad you asked me this question. No, starvation doesn't hurt for a person who's ill and ready to die. It actually brings one to higher consciousness. I didn't feel any pain at all, but my body felt very heavy, like lead. I couldn't lift my leg or turn my head the way I wanted to. My body was like the steering wheel on a car with the control cable disconnected. It was an odd sensation, but it didn't hurt.

ME: What does it feel like to incarnate? Is it attractive to a soul? If life on earth is hard work and misery compared to life in Heaven, what would motivate a soul to come here?

DAN: In the sense of what you understand 'attractive' to mean, no it is not. But try to understand that these decisions are not based on judgments such as, "this experience is good," or "that experience is bad." From a perspective in Heaven, the most exciting, attractive and important thing is the work that will be done in a particular incarnation. The form this work takes on earth -- incarnating in a sick body, or in poverty or with abusive parents -- doesn't feel "good" or "bad" to us from our perspective here. It's only viewed in terms of what it will accomplish and how it will serve our evolution, because souls are naturally motivated to growth.

We are perpetual growth machines, we're creations of creations of creations, and that's what we're made to do. Growth and creation is our only intent and our only interest. The more efficient the form in terms of the work getting done, the better. So a life starving in India as a sick child with no legs looks like a very good idea because it gets a lot done in one incarnation and it serves that particular soul's intention. We in Heaven are aware of how insignificant the body is in the bigger picture, so we think, 'Oh, a body with no legs, that would work well.' One body is not superior or inferior to another. They're just tools, and it's about choosing the right tool for the right job.

Once we get to earth and are subject to human emotions and egos, it all changes. Suddenly a life with no legs doesn't seem like such a good idea anymore. We've lost the elevated perspective from Heaven, and suddenly there is judgment, pain, fear... the whole human experience, which is exactly why we incarnated in the first place, so we could be motivated by that experience to expand and grow. Once on earth we begin to forget about Heaven after three or four years old, and this is actually a good thing, because if we remembered, we'd be completely dysfunctional as humans. We'd be depressed and miserable and want to go back there all the time (many people who are diagnosed as mentally ill are experiencing this syndrome).

THE BREATH MIRROR

On one of my hikes up Cline Butte Danny began talking to me about the "Breath Mirror." This concept knocked my socks off:

"During the last days of my physical life, the days that caused you so much guilt and sadness, I was aware of the emotional chaos around me but was mostly already in Heaven and surrounded by healing. I could see light and peace and healing, as the world of emotions faded into the background. All the sadness I'd felt for you over the years was replaced by a knowledge that was somehow inserted into my consciousness, an awareness of how it feels to release attachment to those dramas and to love all the players equally and unconditionally. I felt great love for Jack even as he was hurting you and Nicole. I could see the beauty of every human thought and action, and I felt a sadness for all the beauty and love that humans on earth aren't aware of. I was being counseled by angels to breathe into my passing, and with each "breath" I could let go with love.

You once asked me about why people have fewer respirations as they die, and this is a good time to explain that. As my body was dying and my breaths were fading and infrequent, there was a mirror image of each breath in Heaven, breathing in new life, in much the same way a baby takes its first breath outside of the womb. With each weakening, struggling breath on earth, a mirror image breath occurs on the other side, getting stronger as each earth breath gets weaker, until the final breath closes one door and opens the other. I was knowing this during the last 24 hours of my physical life, and it required focus and a sort of labor to do that work. I've told you before about the sacredness of breath. This is a good way for people to understand it, as a breath mirror."

I immediately thought about how people sometimes hold a mirror up to the mouth of a dying person to see if they're still breathing, to see if there is breath coming out of the mouth and causing fog on the mirror.

"It's exactly that, a mirror. The whole universe works this way. Heaven is a mirror of life on earth, especially during the early stages of arrival. Breath on earth is sacred, and humans who ignore its importance by living in stressful, toxic environments without spiritual practices, physical exercise or meditation, are taking their breath for granted. In Heaven it's exactly the opposite of that, because during transition from physical life to Heavenly life, it is the breath that carries us through. In Heaven, that same breath is transformed into light and it is our life force here. We don't actually breathe of course because we don't have physical bodies, but what was breath on earth becomes light in Heaven, and we use that light to heal, create and study.

Imagine a reflecting pond. On one side there is breath, on the other side there is light. It is the same thing. In earth life we can learn to use our breath to connect to the light of Heaven and become more empowered in our lives, and this is what the spiritual teachers know and teach. This is why you've found that by doing simple breathing exercises you can hear me and your guides quite easily. And this is also why strong emotion is a barrier to channeling, because emotion squashes and chokes up the breath, clogging up the passageways, as if you're trying to breath through a stuffy nose. You will find that when you are trying to channel and can't because of emotion, breathing deeply and intentionally will help, but not always. First the work has to be done to heal whatever is happening emotionally, so when you are drowning in emotional upheaval (and what happens to breath when you're drowning?), simply say a prayer of gratitude and ask for insight, exactly as you have been doing. You have seen that this always works. It is the only way to healing."

Danny is absolutely correct about how emotions create a barrier to communication with Spirit. When I'm extremely emotional I can't do anything but fret, even when I can feel Danny trying to get my attention. Feeling him hovering around me and being unable to let him in makes me even more upset, and the whole thing spirals into a big ugly pile of angst. Then, to make it even uglier, I feel guilty for not stopping and listening to him, so I throw some guilt into the pile and it pulls me down into even more negative emotion. The only thing that works is prayer, breathing and disciplining myself to sit down and work on this book. Danny comes through easily when I'm writing, perhaps because writing grounds and focuses me so well.

VISITATIONS

Within a year of Danny's passing, Marty, my mother's husband of 30 years and the grandpa referred to earlier, died peacefully in a hospice facility. The family was gathered around him, and during the hours prior to his death I wandered into the little hospice chapel hoping to seek some communion with Danny.

He came to me easily, looking tall, strong and beautiful, and he was happily walking in front of a column of hundreds of people, as if he were leading an army. He told me that these people were Marty's friends and loved ones, members of his soul family from many incarnations, and they were all coming to greet him and lead him home. Danny said that Marty was loved by many, many people, and in past lives he had been a beloved leader. A few months earlier when Marty's body had begun to fail, Danny told me that Marty's mother was hovering close by. During these transmissions I never knew what his mother's name was, but I kept hearing it as "Anna" or "Alma." Months later, when I asked my mother about this, she told me Marty's mother's name was "Ida." I assured my mom that Ida was with Marty, as were many others who love him.

During my visit with Danny in the hospice chapel, he told me that Paula was among the people who'd come to guide Marty. Her purpose there was part of Danny's education in helping people cross over. She was helping Marty, just as she'd helped Danny during his own transition, but in this case she was using Marty to teach Danny about his own role in helping to guide people through. I asked Danny if Marty could see these people, and he said:

> "Yes, he has seen them, but he was afraid of them. It's sad because something in his past gave him a strong fear of death, some negative images and fearful ideas, as many people on earth have. His angel helpers are having a hard time reaching past his fear, but they are present and solid. All you can do from earth is to pray for him to open up to the love of Heaven. He is being met with thousands of loving arms, and passed hand-to-hand from one person to another, like a much-welcomed new baby being handed between one adoring family member and the next. He'll cry with joy when he realizes this great love, and he'll want everyone on earth to know how different it is than what he expected."

SUICIDE

Several months earlier I'd read a book called "Stephen Lives " by Anne Puryear, a woman whose son killed himself at age 15. Shortly after the incident he began communicating with her in much the same way Danny communicates with me, and Danny has brought Stephen into our conversations a time or two, particularly when we're talking about guilt and grief. In one such conversation, I asked them both about suicide, because everything I'd ever read implies that it carries a tremendous karmic weight and negative impact on soul growth. Some even teach that suicide costs extra incarnations and keeps you away from your loved ones on the other side. I've always struggled with this idea because if we plan our lifetimes to serve specific growth plans, then wouldn't suicide also be part of that plan? If we always have free will and can change our plans whenever we choose, then if suicide wasn't in the original plan, it obviously is part of a change of plans, and in that sense, how could it be "wrong?"

Danny and Stephen came together to answer this question for me on more than one occasion. They told me that, for example, Stephen's case was different because he put into his plan that he would die this way as a means of bringing his teachings to the world. Most people don't have that kind of intention tied to their suicides, but Stephen's intention was very high, though it was not realized or expressed until after his death. In fact, the quote on the back of his book says, *"My decision to take my life was wrong Mom, but out of that wrong choice, I have been blessed with a chance to work with you and others, and we have a chance to help others together, from your side and from mine."*

Stephen's book has helped thousands of people, including me, and I'm quite comfortable with the idea of his suicide being part of a soul contract. Danny and Stephen explained it to me as follows:

"Stephen's mother's intense guilt is a vital part of her work on earth. Her process of releasing guilt substantiates the message that every being has its own plan and that nobody can cause another's death. She did not cause or contribute to her son's suicide in any way, but without walking through the fire of guilt she would not have learned this lesson, which was written into her soul's plan. How could one person's plan to be affected by the suicide of a loved one not also involve the loved one's plan to provide the suicide?

Stephen's death had a very high purpose for all involved, and for the thousands of people who've read his book. The reason many teachers think so badly of it -- and you won't hear this very often -- is because they don't want people to use the idea of teaching and soul contracts as an excuse for suicide. It is NEVER the answer to problems or a good way to deal with intense pain. For some people, like Stephen, it serves a higher purpose, while for others it is an act based in fear and perhaps even an aggressive act intended to hurt others. Opportunity to heal the fearful, negative beliefs that motivate a suicide are always offered in Heaven, but it's offered as healing, with great love, and never as punishment. Part of this healing is the choice to create great learning and teaching from this act by helping others, as Stephen has done. God does not judge or punish. God only guides and heals."

In another book written by a mother who communicates with her son from the other side ("Matthew, Tell me About Heaven" by Suzanne Ward), Matthew says that people who come to Heaven via suicide are given the same loving reception and healing energy as any other person, but they enter through a special "treatment station" along with other traumatized souls who need special healing. Matthew says:

It isn't fair or reasonable to lump all suicides into one category with one exacting judgment for all to face up to... whatever their reason, people who commit suicide review their Akashic records with the same self-assessment and next lifetime planning process as any other soul. It's true that they incur an accumulated lesson by having to repeat all the lessons they chose but didn't complete, but there is no punishment or heavy karma levied due to self-inflicted death. Intent or motive is the basis for all determinations of self-judgment, and those people need not judge themselves any more severely than any others in this realm.

Because suicide is so traumatic for the soul and for the loved ones left behind, and because most religions position it as a punishable sin, I was fascinated by the fact that Stephen, Matthew and Danny have a different view that many other spiritual teachers do. I asked Rebecca to present this question to Elishevaa, and found that unlike the others, they view suicide as a dark act that cannot be part of a soul's plan because it's based on the person's belief that he or she is alone and disconnected from divine love. To present a balanced view, I include Elishevaa's comments here:

So often suicide is bound up with enormous dark energy, and most often, instant regret. The soul cries 'what have I done?' and rather than being in a place of peace and seeking the light, feels lost and estranged from God. So often it causes great emotional setback for the soul. This is where prayer is of great assistance, and we do recommend always that ones do pray for those who have taken their own lives, until they feel a sense of peace, a sense of having "broken through." Also, there are angels and guides whose sole work is that of trying to connect with those who are lost, but often their help is rejected for that one feels unworthy of the light. The only exceptions of course are when a suicide takes place by one who is mentally ill, and even that can be difficult from the non-physical. It is a great darkness, this act, and is difficult to describe. Suicide is an act of completely succumbing to illusion. Despair is the active emotion of suicide, and suicide is never an answer, for it causes MORE tangled knots than any problem the one had to begin with. However, we do not want this to be confused with ones who choose to stop medical care, or are making end-of-life decisions, for that is a completely different subject.

GRIEF

There are aspects of Danny's death that I think about non-stop, as if they are happening over and over again on a tape loop. The image of the mortuary people wheeling his body out of the house and of me kissing his head and blessing his brain is etched deeply into my memory. Everything about this image and hundreds like it rip my heart to pieces, and interestingly, the full weight of that pain didn't really hit me until several months after he died. In my journal there's an entry from April 9th, seven months after Danny's death, where I talk about sitting in my little cabin crying and wailing in response to a movie I'd just watched in which a woman's body was carried out of her house by the mortuary people. I must have cried for a full hour, nearly hysterical, and I thought that I was finally beginning to truly deal with my grief, at last.

Looking back on this, I realized that I'd managed to put my grief on hold, postponing it until I'd handled moving, getting divorced and establishing a new life. On a hunch, I checked my files and noted that my divorce was final on March 30th. It was as if I'd held my deepest feelings in abeyance until my connection with Jack was symbolically severed and I felt safe enough to express my feelings again. This is a remarkable lesson in soul contracts and forgiveness.

One of the spiritual gifts Jack gave me was that the crazy dance between us and the stifling energy in our home caused me to shut down emotionally, and this was actually a blessing. If my heart and mind had continued to be susceptible to his disordered energy, I would not have been able to manage Danny's daily care, nor would I have survived two strokes unscathed. My shutting down and withdrawing from Jack was a gift, and now that I'm free and Danny is holding my heart in his hands, it's safe to start feeling again.

At the same time, even in the midst of unbearable grief, I don't actually *miss* Danny. This probably sounds heartless, because for most people dealing with a death, the greatest pain is in the glaring absence of the person they were so close to. But to me, he is not absent at all. He's closer to me now that he was in physical life, and this proves to me over and over again that we humans exist on many levels beyond just the physical, and that love is a life force which vibrates through us all as a connecting fiber, regardless of whether or not we have bodies. Love truly never dies. Here's what Danny has to say about that:

"The reason it feels like you don't miss me is because you and I are a part of each other without boundaries or obstructions. I'm completely IN you, and we are not separated, the same way that God's children are not separated from God. We are un-separated. What you feel with me is a lack of duality. Just like I can't forgive you because I never judged you, you can't miss me because we were never apart. You felt more ripped apart from me when you left me with a babysitter than you do now when I'm in Heaven. All that I am is with you *right now*, and always will be. I am infusing you with love and with information. As an example, when you think of the idea of 'missing' someone, you often think about what it feels like to miss Jack. But in that scenario, it was the drama, familiarity and the deeply ingrained habits that you would actually miss. This chaos shielded you from your divine self. It was very comfortable, and in truth, it was the chaos that you'd really be missing, not Jack himself. The part of you that helped create that chaos, the part of you that created the unhealthy attachment died in the process of separating from him. By contrast, with me there's nothing to miss, because you still have the part of you that created our inter-dimensional relationship, and it doesn't have to die. It's from the light."

This all makes sense, but I still wonder at times why I don't feel as sad, distraught and dysfunctional as I think I'm supposed to feel. I read the websites about grief and what so many other parents describe, and it just isn't the same for me. Sometimes I think I'm just making all this up, and that my communication with Danny is just a strategically contrived fantasy to help me avoid the true pain of his loss. But even as I write those words, I know they aren't true. Elishevaa said that grieving would be different for me than it is for most people, and now I understand why. The only thing that really plagues me is the fear that my communication with Danny might end at some point and I'd have to experience "losing" him all over again.

The moment I had that thought, Danny appeared and said:

"Please don't let thoughts like that cause you to falter. Whenever I feel you doubting this experience I will gently urge you forward, so don't worry. You won't lose me. Your grief is exactly as you've been describing it. You experience me in the form of my essence rather than my body, and it's a thousand times more fulfilling than a body-based relationship. You know intellectually and in your soul that I am closer than ever, because we're sharing the highest possible form of communication.

137

The moments of grief that you feel are very real; the little stabs of loss and pain, the waves of emotion that come up and then recede, are pressure releases and are very healthy for you. Feel them, seek them out if you have to by looking at pictures or listening to music that makes you cry, whatever it takes. Grief is a gateway to Heaven because it holds your heart open, especially if you recognize the loss as your own creation and part of a magnificent plan for your growth.

However, when people are grieving for a loved one, and that grief is tied up with blame, guilt, unworthiness, shame, fear and other emotions that are not based in divine love, it tugs on us here in Heaven, and we reach out to help. We have infinite patience and love of course, but at the same time, their pain summons us to be in the pain with them. We want to assist them, but we can't get through all the negative emotion that comes from their illusion of being separate from God. It ends up separating them from *us* as well. It's important to talk about this in our book because if people on earth understand this, it might serve as a motivation for them to work on releasing those emotions and help them move forward more readily. You will be a great teacher of this truth, through the book and through your hospice work. This experience is purifying you more than you can imagine."

10. How to Heal Yourself and Others

"You can transform illness anytime with the snap of a finger. You can heal yourself instantly if you understand how energy works."

Danny

I've never experienced a year that went by so fast and was so full of personal transformation as the year following Danny's death. Countless lessons have come full circle since the day I made my first entry into the journal that would serve as the raw material for this book. I couldn't have imagined at the time that a year would pass so quickly, and that during that year I would talk to Danny so effortlessly. I also could not have imagined how much my life would change and that I would not only begin to heal, but to actually find joy again. In Danny's infinite wisdom, it is fitting that the final chapter in this book is about healing ourselves and others, because this year was an intense journey of healing for both us.

Although it was our intention to make Part Two of the book more about universal teachings and less about personal experiences, this chapter calls out for reviewing some of my own lessons while sharing the information transmitted from Danny about healing and growth. A year ago I began my struggle to release the patterns and addictions that held me to a destructive relationship. I still grapple with blame and judgment, but it gets easier all the time, and I have Danny, Arlen, my guides and my angels to thank for that. Without their guidance I would not have seen the magic of prayer and forgiveness, nor would I have understood the ease with which we can embrace our experiences -- good or bad -- when we're in alignment with divine energy.

Although the information Danny shares about life, death and healing is always spectacular, one teaching in particular really rocked my reality. It came through in a conversation we had only a few short weeks after his death, while I was struggling mightily with guilt, pain and doubt, and in this dialog he showed me that beings in the spirit realm have *feelings*. They're processing emotions and working as hard on their life stories in Heaven as they did on earth. Contrary to my naive assumption that we're all instantly enlightened the minute we leave our bodies, the hard work doesn't stop the moment we cross over. We carry our growth lessons wherever we go, but in Heaven the information gets processed with less attachment, less ego identity and more love. This was how Danny began teaching me about the different levels on which healing can occur, as evidenced in this journal excerpt from October 2006, about a month after his death:

THE HORSE IN THE CORRAL

I'm on my morning walk at the beach, distraught, depressed, and panicked about what life will be like without Danny. I'm also falling apart under the weight of my decision to leave Jack. Have I done everything I could to work on the relationship? Should I really leave? Is there any hope for healing this marriage?

I suddenly see Danny standing beside Arlen, and Danny looks concerned and upset, which disturbs me greatly, because he usually looks so happy. I can sense that something isn't right, and I wonder, can people on the other side have emotions? I never thought so before, and I feel nervous and worried because Danny is so agitated that Arlen is actually *restraining* him. Danny's trying to pull away, trying to run toward me, but Arlen has him firmly under control. This is baffling, because I've never seen Danny express emotion like this, not even while he was alive on earth. Then it suddenly occurs to me that this is a lesson being taught to Danny, and I've been granted the privilege of observing it.

Danny came to earth disabled and helpless, sacrificing his own physical comfort to be of spiritual service to others. He gave everything of himself, holding back nothing, surrendering completely. But now Arlen is teaching him to hold back. I get the feeling that this is somehow about balance, about learning when to give and when to withhold. Arlen is Danny's teacher, and it seems he's teaching Danny not to give so much. Could that be?

Danny's becoming frantic to reach me, and he wants to soothe me, to intervene in my struggle and ease my pain. At the same moment I realize that I'm watching him learn something in relation to *his own* growth, and that we're learning the mirror image of the same lesson. I'm working on finding my lost voice and acting decisively and with confidence despite my fears and doubts. And on the other side of that mirror, Danny is learning to hold back because he's working on releasing people to find their own way, to not be so much of a teacher, so much of -- dare I say -- a *martyr*. As I'm learning to forge ahead and trust my inner guidance, he's learning to release those he loves to find our own way without taking on our work as his own. In other words, he has control issues just like any other human. Could this be possible?

Until this moment I had the notion that when we leave our bodies we see the folly of our egos and rise above it in an instant. But apparently this is not so. Our souls do their work in many forms, with and without bodies, and there's always more to learn. We are students in Heaven just like we are on earth, but we have more resources and the learning is faster there, because time and space move differently. In Heaven we have the ability to just think about something and the answer just *arrives* (we have this ability on earth too, but it's inhibited by doubt, fear-based religious teachings and other obstructions). We carry with us everything we've created and accumulated through all our lifetimes, and even after we die, we're still in the cycle of birth, death and rebirth until we realize that the cycle is our own choice and our own creation.

As I ponder this, Danny is still trying desperately to reach me, and he's extremely upset. He suddenly morphs into a wild horse held captive in a corral, trying to break free of the ropes that barely contain him, with Arlen as his wrangler. The moment I see that, I instantly realize that the only one who can release him is *me*. Danny put himself into my life with Jack as an energy conductor designed to help me experience the wisdom and choices available in that situation. He gave that to me as a gift of growth, and he is now learning from Arlen to release his attachment to how things turn out. He wants to help me make decisions, to guide me, and Arlen won't let him. He's given himself to me all these years, and now he has to let me go so I can learn on my own. And conversely, on my side of the mirror, my need to keep him as my sole source of love and joy has contributed to holding him in that position. Each of us needs to release the other! So I say this little prayer... *Danny, I release you from having to help me with the decision I'm trying to make right now. You're suffering because I'm calling for you so urgently, and you're responding with your love. But it's time for me to do this work on my own. It's time to release you from having to take care of me. I release you, I release you, and I release you ...*

And immediately the horse image begins to fade and Danny returns to his normal, peaceful state while Arlen retreats into the background.

And Danny says:

"Thank you mom. Releasing our respective roles during these last years together on earth is necessary before you can move forward with your healing. I'm engaged in a similar process here in Heaven, and you will see in the years to come that our relationship will always be changing. The guilt you feel about my suffering during your marriage makes you angry, and you promised yourself that you wouldn't leave until you could process that anger and leave in peace. I will be with you through this process, but it's something you must do on your own. In our physical life I was devoted to helping you learn, and I still am. But now I'm helping in a different manner by letting you find your own way. This is a hard lesson for me too, because I'm so attached to you and to the roles we played in our recent life together. That's why Arlen had to hold me back. You and I are releasing each other from those roles, which frees us to develop new ones, and as a result we will find new ways to work together, such as writing this book. Soon you will no longer think of us as mother and son, as we move forward in our work, together and separately."

THE HEALING COURTYARD

In many of our visits, Danny appears to me in different locations, and one locale is a place I call the *Healing Courtyard*. It looks like a 15th century Italian villa with a lushly landscaped courtyard in the middle. The place is full of flowers, and vines climb along the building's ancient arches. The color of the building is a pale yellow and the light is the same beautiful golden light that appears in Danny's vineyard. Once again, there is the Italy connection, and Danny tells me that we have much history together in Italy, partially tied to Arlen 's work as a teacher in ancient Rome. He told me that we lived an "artistic, esthetic life with much beauty, and even though we were poor, we had music and singing and joy." As an aside, several months after first visiting the courtyard I described it to my friend Odani Keiko, a photographer who travels extensively in Italy. She showed me several photographs of buildings that fit my description, and when I saw the Cloister Garden at the church of San Giovanni in Palermo, I felt strongly that this was the place. I'd never been to Italy (in this incarnation), nor do I recollect ever seeing a picture of that garden before Odani showed it to me.

Danny spoke to me quite often from the Healing Courtyard, where he demonstrated how one soul can help to heal another and how healing energy can easily be transmitted across dimensions. He clarified that he is indeed in a sort of "medical school," learning about energetic healing with a variety of teachers, including our own dear Paula, who, he explained, has been one of his teachers for many lifetimes. He jokingly described her as "a mother who wants her son to be a doctor," and told me that part of the plan for her death at age 46 -- fourteen years prior to his own -- was so that she could prepare to receive him in Heaven.

ME: Tell me more about what you're studying.

DAN: It's more like playing than studying. It's not difficult or stressful like earth schools can sometimes be. We get our lessons from experience and intuition; we can see and feel other beings and we learn through their experiences. We can read the energy of what they did in physical life and what they brought back here to work on. Healing from Heaven is about reading people. I sit in this courtyard with other beings and we telepathically read each other's histories. We can see the wounds and the paths to healing via those wounds, and we heal by sending appropriate colors and light frequencies to each other without a word. This skill is pretty easy in Heaven. Those who have that ability in the physical world studied it here and brought it to earth with them.

There's no physical technology or science to it. It's all about trust, surrender and merging with energy. Here's an example [he shows me a bald man sitting on a bench with him in the courtyard. This man cannot see Danny because this man is actually alive on earth].

In order to send healing to this man I brought his soul here. His earth self isn't even aware of this. We do these healings soul-to-soul. This man is asleep in a hospital right now, having a dream. He's not in a coma or anything, he's just asleep, and in his dream he's sitting with me in the Healing Courtyard. I brought him here so I could look at his energy fields and talk to him about healing himself. It's important to note here that nobody can heal another. The soul that seeks healing has to request it, and this request can usually be made via meditation and prayer. The soul can come here like this and study its issues and intentions. Even if the person is not praying or meditating but the soul still intends healing, it will happen in a dream, or a coma or in a NDE [near-death experience]. The soul will come here to meet with advisors and healers and sit in

143

council. When the body wakes up or returns from meditation, the soul has more information as a result of theses meetings, though this may not be remembered by the person on earth.

However, in some cases it is remembered, for example when people recount what happens during their NDEs. But in most cases people are not aware of their visits to the Heavenly clinic, yet will "miraculously" be healed of their diseases. This is what happens when someone unexpectedly gets cured from a life-threatening illness and the earth doctors can't figure out how it happened. It's really very simple ... the soul decided to heal. You've heard stories of people who are on their deathbeds but they postpone dying until they've had a chance to make peace with an estranged family member. In a scenario like this it often happens that the soul has gone to council and worked with healers on how to die. This work might be done during a dream or meditation, or even in a thought or a daydream that passes so quickly it cannot be remembered. The soul then returns to the body with new knowledge, for example, it remembers that forgiveness is an important part of its plan. It comes to healers in Heaven and says, "I'm about to leave my body but something doesn't feel right. What can I do to create balance here?" And a plan will be made, for example, "Forgive your father for the pain he caused you in this lifetime." And the healing light of forgiveness goes to the father, and the soul agreements kick in for the healing of all.

ME: How are these agreements made? Are healers involved in helping souls make these agreements?

DAN: Yes, it's a vital part of the healing process. For example, I'm working with something you could call soul books, which are the stories of each soul's journey. I help people tune in to their stories to make sure they're on track in terms of doing the work they planned for themselves. I work with a team of advisors, some of whom you've seen at the vineyard. They're members of my soul family, but there are also others who come in for consultation. They bring their own soul families to these councils as well, and people come and go as needed. That's why I have the big vineyard, because it's like a resort with room for everyone. The farm and vineyard isn't growing any physical crops of course, it's just symbolic of planting, growth and harvesting our creations. The process of reviewing these creations and experiences is a big part of healing.

144

I look at the souls and their plans and evaluate them with the team in terms of what would promote the most expansion and healing for each soul. Thinking of these plans as stories or scripts ties in well with the writing of our book, because it's a lot like writing a story (and by the way, part of our plan for this lifetime was that you would be skilled in writing). I'm still an apprentice, and I'm studying with Arlen and others to learn how to help people with their stories. This is another reason why it was important for your personal story to unfold in this book, because it serves as a context, not only for the readers, but also for me as I learn about helping people create the most effective experiences to further their growth. In a sense, our last life together was like a "lab" class in my curriculum.

ME: Carolyn Myss talks a lot about why people don't heal and how it's a choice we make from our souls. If illness is the most perfect way to address a specific lesson, would we also have the choice to work through the lesson and eventually release the illness?

DAN: You can transform illness anytime with the snap of a finger. You can heal yourself instantly if you understand how energy works. You can look at why you're clinging to your illness, and you might see that you're holding onto it because it keeps you locked into beliefs and actions that validate your illusion that you are separate from God, such as blame, powerlessness and victimhood. Not many people can look at that, but if someone can, he may no longer need the illness. You actually know several people who have chronic medical complaints that at times seem like obsessions. These illnesses were created many lifetimes ago as defense mechanisms, either for protection from a harmful situation or in response to trauma. The people I speak of have made these illnesses an intrinsic part of their identities, and broadcast them constantly, which keeps the illnesses in place. The illnesses now serve the same purpose they did when they were originally manifested; they generate a lot of attention and keep people and intimate experiences at a distance. It is absolutely possible to change these illnesses, but it takes a lot of work, time and a willingness to face the fearful places. Reading, counseling, meditating, opening the chakras and asking for help from guides are just a few of the methods that can be used to begin the process.

ME: But some of the people you mention already do this work, yet still cling to their illnesses.

145

DAN: This is where the soul's intention prevails. Disease can be chosen to further the soul's work and as a means to healing others. For example, your friend who was just diagnosed with Leukemia was once the "black sheep" of her family, but now she has become a healing light at the center of the family. Everyone around her is transforming because of her illness, and this is a gift she's giving to them, in the same way my illness was a gift to you. Healing doesn't necessarily mean the elimination of illness. It can also be the release of the body to death, which transforms the person who dies as well as the people around him.

Emotional healing can be triggered by many types of transitions, such as losing a relationship or a job. The life of the soul is never static, it's always moving forward. Most illness and pain comes from the ego's resistance to that forward motion. You could almost call it "motion sickness." Pain and illness are ways for the soul to say to the ego, "There's something that needs our attention. Let's look at it and see how we can work with it." Healing is about learning to listen to these messages and taking action.

For example, your friend Amanda has alienated her friends and family with her many ailments and her incessant complaints and demands. Her husband has wanted to leave her for years, but he stays because of the exquisitely crafted dance between them, which he interprets as an obligation to care for her and keep her "happy." She says she wants to heal, but she isn't looking at the deeper questions. Instead of saying to herself, "Why am I so miserable?" the better question to ask would be, "How do these illnesses serve me?" If she'd examine the way she uses her ailments to control others, she could begin to heal.

We are always free to choose a different path. Amanda is not choosing physical health because it would require her to dismantle a structure she established with her family years ago. To break this structure down would not only shift her reality, it would shift all the others in her family, and this would cause tremendous change -- and growth -- for everyone. But the ego is always more comfortable staying where it is, especially if it's experiencing the illusion of control. What most people don't realize is that once you set foot on the path to truth, the pain of facing your fears is fleeting, but the joy of growth is everlasting."

MOTION SICKNESS

Most of this book was written in the Spring and Summer of 2007, following my arrival in Oregon. It was a powerful time for me, having leapt from dizzying heights off the precipice, trusting that Spirit would carry me. I spent more time alone than I ever had in my life, with no partner or child to love or care for, only my own soul, which was demanding my undivided attention. During this time I was blessed with a stable income that allowed me to work at home as a freelance writer and marketing consultant, and my days were filled with peace, creativity, exercise, meditation and the support of a new tribe of spiritually aware friends. It was a golden period in my life, and Danny was very much a part of it.

But there were also days when I got clobbered by the irreparable break in my heart. I'd lost my beautiful son, my role as a mother, my job as a caregiver, my husband, my stepdaughter, my home in Alabama and even my little dog Jackson. I'd also discovered that within weeks of my departure, Jack was deeply ensconced in a new romance. Over the months I made several attempts to make peace with him by sending emails offering friendship, support and forgiveness, but he ignored them all. Mutual friends report that he never asks about me or even mentions my name. There is still a lot of grieving to be done.

Whenever I'm in the midst of this kind of heartache, I find it difficult to meditate, pray or tune in to spirit at all, and at these times I feel more lonely than ever, because it seems that even my disembodied friends have abandoned me. I've learned from my spiritual studies that there's no way around these feelings and that the best thing to do is to *breathe into* them and let them engulf me completely. Feeling the full range and stinging clarity of the pain is necessary before it can be released to the light for transformation and learning.

In assembling this chapter on healing, Danny led me back to journal entries that beautifully illustrate his amazing teachings, and he drew me toward those in which I'd felt the most disheartened, depressed, hopeless, worthless and unlovable. In the spirit of providing a context for these teachings, I quote some of them here.

March 22

I've been feeling tired, hopeless, sad and lonely the last few days, and I can't identify the feeling. I'm edgy and can't sit still, and even when I walk down the canyon to my meditation spot, I pace back and forth like a caged animal. Why can't I just sit on a rock and be still, even for 60 seconds? I pray for help with stillness, because I can feel that something's off, something's not balanced. I discipline myself to do the chakra visiting meditation and notice immediately that the problem area is my heart. I see a gaping, bleeding wound there, something I'd avoided looking at until this moment. I can sense that my guides want me to look at the origin of this wound, and the feeling of discomfort is so powerful that I know it's important, so I get my little digital voice recorder and start praying and meditating out loud, recording what I see and hear.

The first wound that comes to my awareness is the chronic rejection and dismissal I experienced at the hands of my husband, and the realization that he never actually loved me. All the times he passionately proclaimed his devotion, all the times he begged to reunite after our many breakups, it wasn't *love* at all. It was his black hole of emotional starvation, and I could pour everything I had into that hole, including my fragile son, but it would always be empty. Yet he will never actually starve, because he'll always find someone new to sign on as a source of narcissistic supply. It turns out I meant nothing to him, and this realization cut me to the core.

I continue look at my heart and I see green, the color of the heart chakra, but my heart looks like a malformed bell pepper, and I'm seeing little sewing stitches all around it. It's a funny picture, and I thank Danny for making me laugh. It looks like a comic book drawing, with green spikey sound effect bubbles saying "Bam, Boom" like in the old comics when two superheroes duke it out. I meditate on my heart as something beaten up in a battle between superpowers. But I don't want to simply stitch up the wound; I just want to open it and infuse it with peace. I ask for healing light, and the light around my green pepper heart slowly, gently turns pink. There is illumination and forgiveness almost instantly.

I thank Danny for showing me how to do this healing work, and he says:

"This is an example of how prayer is always effective. When you feel sad or uncomfortable, you take it to Spirit, you eek out a time, carve out a niche, get a tape recorder or a pencil and speak your need. The reason you have discomfort is because messages are

148

trying to get to you, somebody's calling you. To get over that edge you have to tune in and ask, open up and receive the messages and record them, and you'll move past the discomfort. The discomfort is a knock on your door. It's your psychic cell phone ringing. Don't ever hesitate to do this for yourself, because every healing you do on yourself has an effect on the collective. The more you do this work on yourself the more it will help others.

Practice healing by visiting the courtyard. You can summon any soul to come to you, including your own. Emotional wounds are alive and organic. Honor them and they will lead you to new information and experiences that will open up new layers of awareness and renewed waves of healing. This is the value of our wounds, to keep us focused on the healing realms. This is how you learn to resonate more light and to operate at a higher frequency, generating waves of light like a beacon, like a transmitter to God. And you'll find that you can receive waves back, which gives you power for healing others.

Without open wounds this couldn't happen. The idea is not to stitch up and seal off your wounds. This idea is to keep them accessible for healing energy, to ventilate them, like putting a gauze pad over a cut, just enough covering to keep it from getting infected, but still letting air through the mesh. Air and light are the same thing, and that's why breath is so important. When you work with breath you're working with light."

May 22

Tonight I received a long, beautiful, much-needed message from Danny. It began earlier in the day when I was hiking and worrying about not getting the book done fast enough. He said:

"Do not worry about the speed at which you produce the book. Everything you're doing with your time right now is part of your healing, and you can't move any faster than your healing will allow. Remember that in the moments when you're withdrawn from the world you are NOT withdrawn from Spirit. These are times of mourning and awakening for you, and you must honor that. Notice how your prayers ask for insight rather than comfort. This is good work. Everything you're experiencing now is for the book, especially the parts that feel shameful or embarrassing, like your struggle in releasing Jack and the bitterness and anger you feel at times. You

149

are exploring your humanity and your vulnerability. People who read this book need to see your fragility, and to know that you're vulnerable just like they are. This is your lesson in humility, as Carolyn Myss describes in one of your favorite books.

When you do something that you perceive as 'stupid' or 'weak,' it keeps your feet on the earth and helps you acknowledge your human foibles and limitations. You have tried to be too strong for too long, and your devotion to spiritual practice makes it even more complicated, because at times you're so busy being spiritual that you don't allow yourself to be human. You can't write a book from Heaven without allowing the experience of human vulnerability to walk with you every step of the way."

THE LITTLE ENGINE THAT COULD

April 12

Today was a sad day. I'm trying to focus on allowing myself to collapse into the arms of the angels, but my tough exterior makes it quite a challenge. I can hear Danny telling me over and over again, "Just lie down with me, let me hold you, don't expect words. This is one of the times when the greatest peace and highest healing can occur just by sitting in my presence."

He takes me into the healing courtyard and I see myself sitting there like a lost puppy, beaten, starving and abandoned. And then he shows me an image of myself hatching through an egg, the same sort of egg he moved through at his death, and I'm shedding a skin or membrane of some sort. I'm covered in birth goo, and Danny tells me that the sadness I'm feeling is a labor pain. I'm giving birth to my Self, just like he was reborn when he passed through to Heaven. He's holding my head like a midwife does when she catches a baby. He's literally *midwifing* me into my new life.

He tells me that I'm frail like a newborn baby and that I need to stop standing up so resolutely and start nurturing myself with extreme care. He says there was a layer of coating over me that's now thinning. It was a coating that protected me from the raw pain of my grief, and it created a cocoon necessary to help me deal with his death, the ending of my marriage and my move into a new life. But now it's time to step out into much stronger light. During this time of transformation, the protective layer is so thin that there is absolute exposure, and the light of truth hits this exposed, raw Self with great pain, similar to what it feels like when air comes in contact with skin that has been burned. Danny tells me that the angels will provide my protection from now on, rather than the false protection of denial, distraction and diversion (the 3 Ds) that I've relied on in the past. He tells me to ask my guides to lift and carry me through this "pupa" while shedding and rebuilding my new skin. I look up the word "pupa" in the dictionary and it says: *The non-feeding stage between the larva and adult in the metamorphosis of holometabolous insects, during which the larva typically undergoes complete transformation within a protective cocoon or hardened case.*

April 13

Tonight I had a surprisingly intense encounter with Danny during another mediumship circle with Mariah Crawford. I saw him in the Healing Courtyard, and the place was lit up with party lights. I sensed they were having a party because they were so excited that Mariah had contacted them. There was a bit of dialog that I don't recall, but the most important part was Danny showing me an image of my heart chakra. Anchoring this image was a tiny, vulnerable heart, live and vibrant and clear and green. It was surrounded by dark, rusted old machinery, the kind you might see in an old factory. There were giant gears turning and churning everywhere, and my little heart was in the midst of them, chugging along with great effort, trying to keep pace with the machines, gasping for air and on its last legs, but working with great determination.

And Danny said, "Your heart is like the train in the children's book, *'The Little Engine That Could,'* pushing up the hill endlessly. I want you to take a break from forgiving everybody and working so hard to be non-judgmental. It's time to truly feel your pain, your power, and even your anger. You must clear these things from your heart before you can really move forward in healing yourself and others."

This was the saddest image I could ever have imagined for my heart chakra, and I sent it love, light and prayers to free it from its stress and strain while meditating on Danny's words. Could it be true that I can simply relax and not expect so much of myself? I'd worked so hard all my life to be brilliant and accomplished, to be strong, smart, confident and *in control*. I'd lived so much of my life in *my will*, and the idea of surrendering that control seemed terrifying. But I knew it was time for me to take Danny's words to heart, literally.

Over the next couple of months I sank into a period of deep despair, and grappled with guilt, depression, anger, loneliness, unemployment and health problems. It was as if these things showed up on cue in preparation for the next phase of my transformation. And it was no accident that I was involved in the Anamcara training during this period, because it gave me valuable tools -- like ritual, prayer and music -- that were vital to my healing.

One day I was in so much psychic pain that I asked Mariah to help me through it. It was not long after my guilt attack at the Anamcara seminar, and I was still struggling with the memories of the day Jack behaved so monstrously in front of Danny. My guilt was eating me alive. Mariah came over to give me some much-needed spiritual support. We walked with Henry down to the river and stood in the middle of the medicine wheel I'd built there, invoking the four directions and calling Danny to come to us. Henry busied himself being a dog, running around playing, alternately rolling in the mud and jumping into the river. Danny showed up instantly (he loves talking to Mariah) and said:

"If I'd been a normal kid I would have stood up to Jack, maybe pushed or shoved him, or physically intervened in some way. I would have protected you and tried to make you leave. But I couldn't protect you, and you'll be surprised to know that I felt guilty too. Sick and dying people have guilt about many things, such as being a burden, draining the family finances and causing emotional pain for their loved ones. All the time you were loving me and caring for me, you were suffering terribly, and it nearly killed you. If I hadn't required so much attention you might have been able to deal with Jack more easily, or perhaps left him sooner.

When I tell you that I feel guilty about this, you say, 'Oh no Danny, it was an honor and a pleasure to care for you. Please don't feel guilty!' Well, that's exactly how I feel when you tell me about your guilt. Consider the guilt balanced between us, so we can both move on and zero out our respective guilt accounts. You can see the absurdity of my having felt guilty, and how needless it was, so in seeing that in me, you can hopefully see it in yourself as well. Guilt is something we all need to wash off, just like Henry washes the mud off himself in the river. Before the mud of guilt dries and sets, we must cleanse ourselves in healing waters to be free of it. Guilt is a plague in civilization."

This piece of wisdom was an incredible healing tool for me. Guilt is clearly the enemy of healing, and I can see how this related to my Anamcara studies and the work I was doing with hospice patients. But what Danny said about guilt being a plague in civilization fascinated me more than anything else, and several days later I asked him about it again. He said:

"It has everything to do with our separation from God. Humans have an innate attraction to guilt because we left Heaven and, as the Course in Miracles states, the moment we found ourselves separate we began struggling to get back home. We had lost the knowledge that says, "getting back home is instant, you arrived on earth with the tools and the abilities to connect to home any time." But we were so deeply steeped in grief about leaving that this idea did not come through easily. The pain of being in bodies and the loss of light was so great that the emotional energy of grief prevented us from communicating with Heaven, and we grieved for this loss. This is the true source of human guilt. Corrupt religious politics knew how to latch onto this and used it to control people.

To return to a state of balance where guilt can be released entirely, humans on earth need to understand that they're grieving for Heaven, and that this grief should be processed just as they would process grief for any separation—divorce, death, loss of a job, a home, etc. Those things represent leaving Heaven. It's a divorce from our divine state, the death of an identity and the loss of our jobs as creators. The concept of 'loss' only exists because we believe we are truly separate from God, which we are NOT.

This is what spiritual work teaches us. Not to learn anything new, but to remember what we already know. We come into this world as newborns in much the same way we came to physical life when we first left our home in Heaven. Every time a baby is born it repeats this process of separation, and the soul of a baby is born grieving for Heaven. In a sense we're born with guilt, because we're very much aware of the pain of separation the moment we're born. But guilt isn't really an accurate word. It's more like a longing to make things right. A sense that something is out of alignment. If you think about the times when you've felt guilt, you'll see that it feels as if you've dishonored your soul or someone else's. It's a feeling that you are offset from your soul, or out of synch.

Some guilt does have a purpose, for example, when one intentionally harms another for greed or power, such as robbery, rape or abuse. In these situations guilt opens a window for healing and transformation. But that's not the guilt we're speaking of. We're talking about feeling guilty even though you offered your purest and highest love and acted in accordance with God, yet still feel that you've done something 'wrong.' This is needless guilt.

During the days surrounding my death, you felt guilty because you could not create the scene you wanted, you could not command the environment or control what happened, and you felt like you failed to properly serve me, yourself and God. In order to heal this guilt, you must remember that we are always serving God, ourselves and our soul families, no matter what happens. We're acting out our soul contracts, and every soul is in perfect agreement with the scenario. If you could see the scene with Heavenly eyes there would be no guilt at all, only joy that agreements were being fulfilled. If it had not happened the way it did, we would not be having this conversation now, and you wouldn't be armed with this information to share with your hospice families and the people who read this book. Can you see how it spreads, like a network that includes everybody touched by the experiences and by the sharing of them? We're all in this together. Not only are we not separated from God, we are not separated from each other."

BUILDING MY HOUSE OF LOVE

As this chapter comes to a close (literally and figuratively), it seems that an epilogue of sorts is in order. My dog Henry is still alive and well, and as of this writing still plays happily along the riverbank and has not been run over by a truck. I'm deeply involved in the Anamcara project and have hospice patients with whom I visit regularly (I can see angels hovering around all of them). My world widens by degrees each day, and other than sore ankles from hiking up and down the canyon, my health is stable. There is no man in my life, and the reason for this is twofold: I'm somewhat traumatized about relationships and have a lot more work to do in that area, and I'm actually enjoying this time alone. I know however, without a doubt, that there's an aware, awake, emotionally healthy man being prepared for me at this very moment, on his way down the pike headed straight for my heart. And I'm willing to wait.

I'm now living in my new house in Sisters, Oregon, a house I *built*, despite the fact that toward the end of construction my income dwindled down to practically zero, and for a while I worked as a hotel maid to make ends meet. After I got over he initial shock of my two biggest clients canceling their contracts in the same month, I turned to Spirit for an explanation and as always, the answers were crystal clear.

It was time for me to put my money where my mouth was, and to dedicate myself to my work as a spiritual teacher and channel for Danny, which required me to live on absolute faith in my soul's intention. I can feel the manifestation energy at work at this very moment as I commit these words to paper. This was not only meant to be a time of trusting that my soul knows exactly what it's doing, it was also a gift to help me finally let go of the past. One of the two departed clients was one I'd shared with Jack for six years, and even though Jack had a malevolent hand in taking that job from me, I was *grateful*. It was the last vestige of my connection to him, and it freed me in a hundred small ways. All the snapping of rubber bands around my wrist didn't accomplish in a year what losing that client did in one day. I even went down to the river and shot one of my rubber bands across the water.

I won't be needing rubber bands anymore.

God only *gives*

"Swans sing before they die- 'twere no bad thing, should certain persons die before they sing"

Samuel Taylor Coleridge

ABOUT THE AUTHORS

Terri Daniel began her career as an author and lecturer in 1990, when, under her previous name, Terri Mandell, she published her first book, *POWER SCHMOOZING: The New Etiquette for Social and Business Success.* The book touted a radical new approach to social networking, and replaced traditional notions of "proper" etiquette with brazen, in-your-face strategies for creating deeper, more honest social and business connections.

Terri spent six years teaching and lecturing on the seminar circuit, conducting Power Schmoozing workshops for groups that encompassed every imaginable lifestyle and industry, from Fortune 500 CEOs to starving artists. She was a frequent guest on television and radio talk shows and was featured in hundreds of magazines and newspapers. Her follow up book, *When Good People Throw Bad Parties: A Guide to Party Politics for Hosts and Guests,* attracted a cult following of socialites and party planners, and kept her busy with media appearances, consulting and lecturing throughout the 1990s.

But by 1999, after a divorce and the diagnosis of her nine year-old son Danny with a life-threatening illness, the trappings of the fast lane lost their appeal and Terri headed for a major lifestyle change.

She immersed herself in metaphysical study and became ordained as a Spiritual Humanist minister. She supported herself and Danny as a marketing consultant and copywriter, supplementing her income and exercising her intuitive and public speaking skills with Tarot readings and unconventional wedding ceremonies.

In 2005 Terri moved with Danny and her new husband Jack to a small southern town, where she quickly became popular as a spiritual teacher, conducting classes and workshops on meditation, manifestation, divination and channeling. Terri continues to facilitate metaphysical study groups and recently began working as an "11th Hour" hospice volunteer (supporting patients in the process of active dying). She also counsels bereaved parents throughout the U.S., offering alternative perspectives on disability, death and loss. She has spoken on the topic of conscious death to community groups, churches and at spiritual conferences, and her articles have been published in numerous magazines and websites.

Danny Snowden-Mandell was born in 1990 and adopted at birth by Terri and her then-husband. As a healthy, happy young boy, Danny loved Pokemon, swimming, downhill skiing, fighter jets, Lego models and James Bond. Girls and women adored him, and he excelled at reading, storytelling and video games.

In 1998 he began exhibiting unusual physical and cognitive symptoms, and was diagnosed two years later with a rare metabolic disorder called *Metachromatic Leukodystrophy*, which eventually robbed Danny of his motor skills and his ability to speak.

Danny was -- and still is -- a smart, funny, spiritually advanced, remarkable human being who left the earth plane at age 16. He was a teacher and guide to all who knew him, but the greatest honor of all was that he began speaking to his mother telepathically from the Other Side almost immediately after his death.

This book is the result of those conversations.

To order additional copies of

A SWAN IN HEAVEN:
Conversations Between Two Worlds

Please contact the publisher:

FIRST HOUSE

PRESS

359 N. Locust Lane
Sisters, OR. 97759
(541) 549-4004

www.SwanInHeaven.com

CPSIA information can be obtained
at www.ICGtesting.com
Printed in the USA
LVHW031438270120
644902LV00001B/61